Analog Communication Handnote

Prepared by

Md. Ariful Islam

Faculty Member

Department of Robotics and Mechatronics Engineering

University of Dhaka

Email: arif.rme@du.ac.bd

<u>Table of Contents</u>   **<u>Page</u>**

Chapter-1: Fundamental Concepts

Chapter-2: Radio Wave Propagation

Chapter-3: Amplitude Modulation

Chapter-4: Frequency Modulation

Chapter-9: Television

CHAPTER-1
FUNDAMENTAL CONCEPTS

1.1 WHAT IS COMMUNICATION?

Communication can be defined as the process of exchange of information through means such as words, actions, signs, etc., between two or more individuals.

1.2 WHAT IS ANALOG COMMUNICATION?

The communication based on analog signals and analog values is known as Analog Communication.

1.3 ELEMENTS OF A WIRELESS COMMUNICATION SYSTEM

The most basic possible wireless system consists of a transmitter, a receiver, and a channel, usually a radio link, as shown in figure.

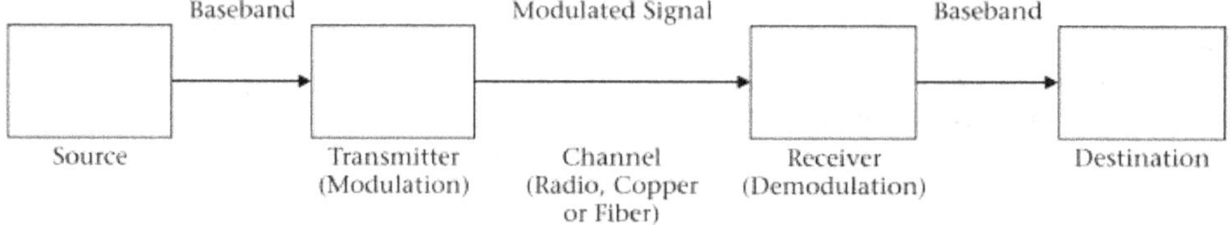

Fig: Elements of a communication system

➢ **Source:** Provides information. The source of the information signal can be analog or digital. Typical examples are video, audio, and digital data.
   Sources may be described by the frequency range they occupy
   - o Telephone-quality frequency range is 300 Hz - 3 kHz
   - o Music frequency range is 20 Hz - 20 kHz
   - o Video requires a frequency range from dc to 4.2 MHz
➢ **Baseband:** The information signal is sometimes called the intelligence, the modulating signal, or the baseband signal.
➢ **Modulation:** The process by which some characteristic of a carrier is varied by an information signal. Usually, the carrier is a sine wave. In modulation, any one of the following parameters (characteristics) of the carrier signal can be varied with respect to time are: Frequency, Amplitude and Phase. The carrier frequency is much higher than the highest frequency component of the information signal.
   A general equation of a typical carrier signal is given by

$$e(t) = E_c \sin(\omega_c t + \theta)$$

where,

$e(t)$ = instantaneous carrier voltage

E_c = peak voltage of the carrier

ω_c = frequency of the carrier in radians per second

t = time

θ = phase angle in radians

> **Modulated Signal:** The signal after modulation process is called modulated signal.
> **Channel:** By which a signal is passed from transmitter to receiver. A communication channel can be a pair of conductors, Fiber-optic cable or Radio Frequency.
> **Demodulation:** The inverse process, demodulation, is performed at the receiver in order to recover the original information.
> **Destination:** Where the signal has to be reached.

An ideal communication system would reproduce the information signal exactly at the receiver. Any other changes constitute distortion.

1.4 Simplex, Half and Full Duplex Communication

Simplex:

It is one way communication. For example- Printer, Email etc.

Full Duplex:

Sometimes communication can take place in both directions at once. This is called full-duplex communication (Figure). An ordinary telephone call is an example of full-duplex communication. It is quite possible (though perhaps not desirable) for both parties to talk at once, with each hearing the other.

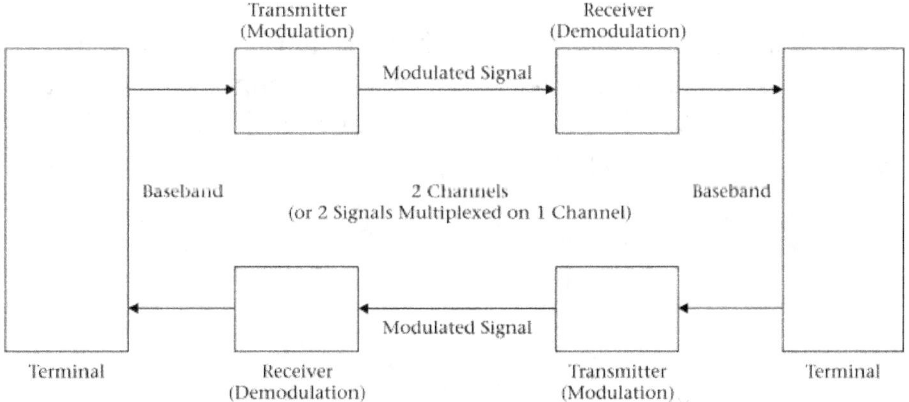

Fig: Full-duplex communication system

Half Duplex:

Some two-way communication systems do not require simultaneous communication in both directions. An example of this half-duplex type of communication is a conversation over citizens' band (CB) radio. The operator pushes a button to talk and releases it to listen. It is not possible to talk and listen at the same time, as the receiver is disabled while the transmitter is activated (Figure 3). Half-duplex systems save bandwidth by allowing the same channel to be used for communication in both directions. They can sometimes save money as well by allowing some circuit components in the transceiver to be used for both transmitting and receiving.

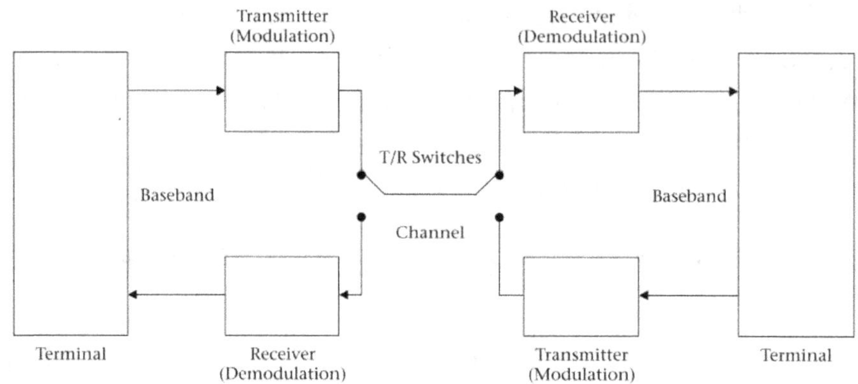

Fig: Half-duplex communication system

1.5 CITIZENS' BAND (CB) RADIO:

CB radio is a short-distance unlicensed radio communication system.

1.6 WHAT IS SIGNAL?

Carry useful information.

1.7 WHAT IS NOISE?

Noise is an unwanted signal, which interferes with the original message signal and corrupts the parameters of the message signal. This alteration in the communication process, leads to the message getting altered. It most likely enters at the channel or the receiver. The noise signal can be understood by taking a look at the following figure 4.

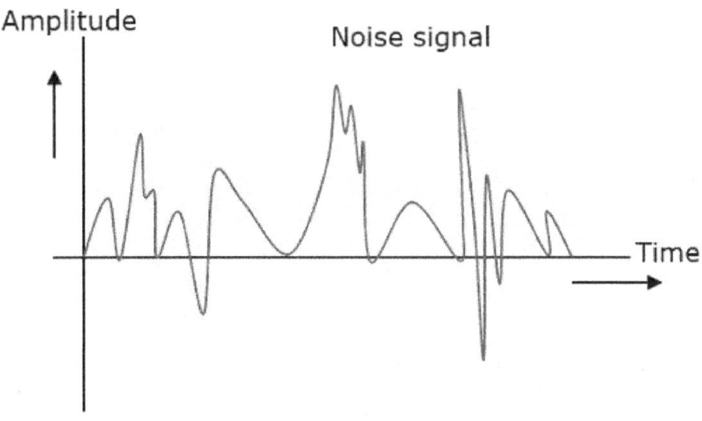

Fig: Noise

Hence, it is understood that the noise is some signal which has no pattern and no constant frequency or amplitude. It is quite random and unpredictable. Measures are usually taken to reduce it, though it can't be completely eliminated. Most common examples of noise are −

i.   Hiss sound in radio receivers
ii. Buzz sound amidst of telephone conversations
iii. Flicker in television receivers, etc

1.7.1 TYPES OF NOISE

Noise is classed one of two ways: External noise and Internal noise

1. External Noise:

External noise is interference added to a signal from a channel (such as radio channel) or from an equipment (such as car engines, light dimmers, vacuum cleaners or even computers). Even solar flare from the sun can affect electronic communication on earth.

External noise types:

➤ Equipment noise
➤ Atmospheric noise
➤ Space noise

2. Internal Noise

Internal noise is generated in all electronic equipment. Passive components (such as resistors and cables) and active devices (such as diode and transistors) can be noise sources.

Internal noise types:

- ➢ Thermal noise
- ➢ Shot noise
- ➢ Partition noise
- ➢ Excess noise (flicker noise)
- ➢ Transit-time noise

DEFINITION OF SOME NOISE

1. **Thermal noise:** Random motion of electrons in a wire.
2. **Crosstalk:** Effect of one wire on the other.
3. **Induced noise:** Comes from sources such as motors and appliances.
4. **Impulse noise:** Spike that comes from power lines and lighting.
5. **White noise:** Noise power is proportional to Bandwidth. It contains all frequencies. Noise power density is $P_N = kTB$
6. **Shot noise:** Occurs in transistor and diode.
7. **Flicker noise:** Occurs in low frequency.
8. **Pink noise:** Light is pink when it contains more red in low frequency.

1. Thermal Noise:

Thermal noise is a kind of internal noise that is produced by the random motion of electrons in a conductor due to heat. This type of noise is found everywhere in electric and electronic circuitry. The power density of thermal noise is constant with frequency, i.e., equal power in every hertz of bandwidth. So this is called white noise.

Noise power equation:
$$P_n = kTB$$

P_n = Noise power in watts;
k = Boltzmann's constant
T = Absolute temperature in kelvins;
B = Noise power bandwidth in Hertz

Noise voltage equation:
$$V_N = \sqrt{4kTBR}$$

Problem-1.1: A resistor at a temperature of 25°C is connected across the input of an amplifier with a bandwidth of 50 kHz. How much noise does the resistor supply to the input of the amplifier?

First we have to convert the temperature to kelvins.
From Equation (1.4),

$$T(K) = T(°C) + 273$$
$$= 25 + 273$$
$$= 298 \text{ K}$$

Now substitute into Equation (1.3),

$$P_N = kTB$$
$$= 1.38 \times 10^{-23} \times 298 \times 50 \times 10^{3}$$
$$= 2.06 \times 10^{-16} \text{ W}$$
$$= 0.206 \text{ fW}$$

6. Shot Noise:

- **Shot noise** is a type of electronic noise which originates from the discrete nature of electric charge.
- The noise is due to random variations in current flow in active devices such as tubes, transistors and semiconductor diodes.
- The device current is a flow of carriers such as electrons or holes, each of which carries a finite amount of charge.
- The name shot noise describes the random arrival of electrons like individual shots from a shot gun.

Noise current equation for for a junction diode:

$$I_N = \sqrt{2kI_oB}$$

1.7.2 EFFECTS OF NOISE

Noise is an inconvenient feature, which affects the system performance. Following are the effects of noise.

1. Noise limits the operating range of the systems

Noise indirectly places a limit on the weakest signal that can be amplified by an amplifier. The oscillator in the mixer circuit may limit its frequency because of noise. A system's operation depends on the operation of its circuits. Noise limits the smallest signal that a receiver is capable of processing.

2. Noise affects the sensitivity of receivers

Sensitivity is the minimum amount of input signal necessary to obtain the specified quality output. Noise affects the sensitivity of a receiver system, which eventually affects the output.

1.8 DISTORTION

Any changes in the baseband signal are referred to as distortion.

1.8.1 TYPES OF DISTORTION

Some types of distortion are:

- Inter-modulation distortion
- Harmonic distortion
- Nonlinear frequency response
- Nonlinear phase response
- Noise
- Interference

1.8.2 REASONS OF DISTORTION

1. Creation of harmonics of baseband frequencies f_b
2. f_b mixing with each other
3. Phase shift of f_b

DIFFERENCE BETWEEN DISTORTION AND NOISE

I. Distortion is a change of the original signal, whereas noise is an external random signal added to the original signal.
II. Removing the effects of noise is harder than removing the effects of distortion.
III. Noise has a more stochastic nature compared to distortion.

1.9 ATTENUATION

Attenuation by word means to get weak (Figure).

When a signal travels through a medium its energy is lost, resulting in decrease in the amplitude of the wave i.e. with the distance of propagation the strength of the signals becomes weak and this phenomenon is known as attenuation.

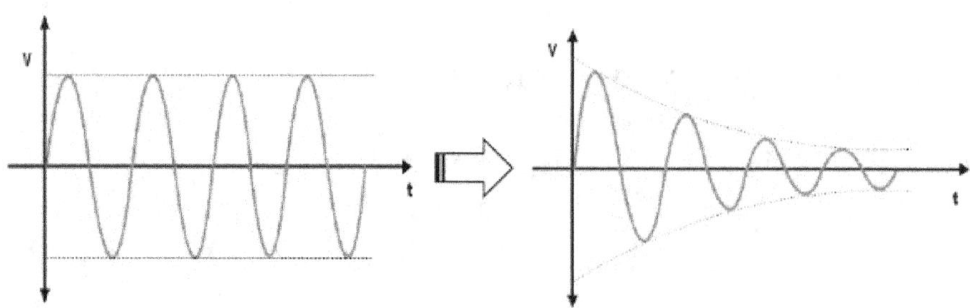

Fig: Attenuation

Attenuation is a natural phenomenon that cannot be prevented while transmitting signals but we can use repeater to amplify the signal again.

1.10 WHAT IS BANDWIDTH?

The range of frequencies is called bandwidth. In other words, the portion of frequency spectrum occupied by a signal is called bandwidth.

$$BW = f_2 - f_1$$

1.11 WHAT IS SNR?

$$SNR = \frac{Signal\ Power}{Noise\ Power} = \frac{P_S}{P_N}$$

This SNR is usually expressed in decibels is one of the most important characteristics of a communication system. The larger the SNR is, the better the system is.

1.12 NOISE FIGURE (NF)

Noise figure describes the way in which a device adds noise to a signal and thereby degrades the signal-to-noise ratio. It is defined as follows:

$$NF = \frac{(S/N)_i}{(S/N)_o}$$

where

$(S/N)_i$ = signal-to-noise ratio at the input

$(S/N)_o$ = signal-to-noise ratio at the output

All of the above are expressed as power ratios, not in decibels. Since thermal noise is produced by all conductors and active devices, it follows that any stage in a communication system will add noise. When a device has multiple stages, each stage contributes noise, but the first stage is the most important because noise inserted there is amplified by all other stages. The equation that expresses this is:

$$NF_T = NF_1 + \frac{NF_2 - 1}{A_1} + \frac{NF_3 - 1}{A_1 A_2} + \cdots$$

where

NF_T = total noise figure for the system

NF_1 = noise figure of the first stage

NF_2 = noise figure of the second stage

A_1 = gain of the first stage

A_2 = gain of the second stage

1.13 Equivalent Noise Temperature

Equivalent noise temperature is another way of specifying the noise performance of a device. Noise temperature has nothing to do with the temperature of the device; it is the absolute temperature of a resistor, that connected to the input of a noiseless amplifier, would produce the same noise at the output as the device under discussion.

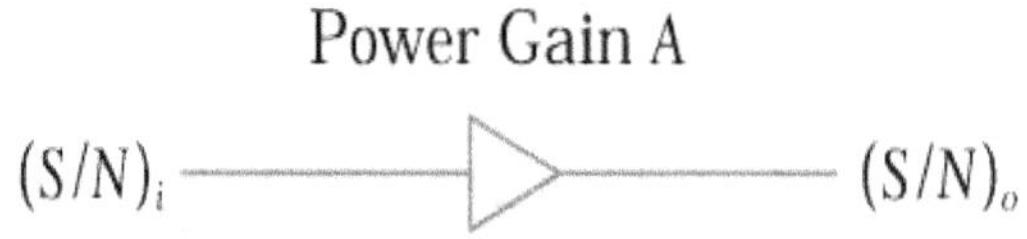

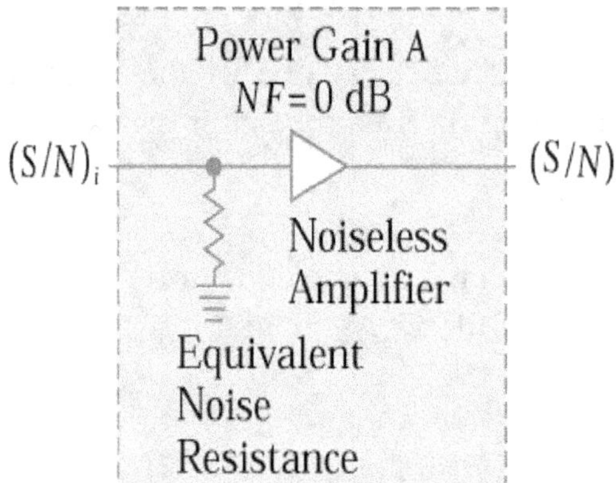

Fig: Equivalent Noise Resistance

1.14 Cascaded Amplifiers

When two or more amplifiers are connected in cascade, the noise figure of the first stage is the most important in figuring the noise performance of the entire system because the noise generated there is amplified in all succeeding stages (Figure).

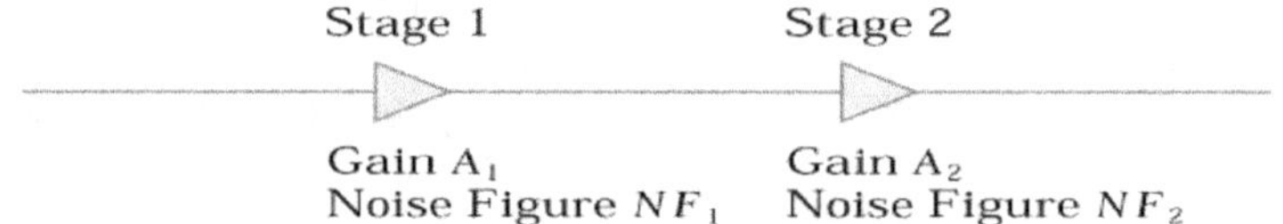

Fig: Cascaded amplifiers

1.15 Noise Figure to Noise Temperature

Converting noise figure to noise temperature is quite easy:

$$T_{eq} = 290(NF - 1)$$

where

$$T_{eq} = \text{equivalent noise temperature in kelvins}$$
$$NF = \text{noise figure as a ratio (not in dB)}$$

Problem-1.2: *A three-stage amplifier has stages with the following specifications. Gain and noise figure are given as ratios.*

Stage	Power Gain	Noise Figure
1	10	2
2	25	4
3	30	5

Calculate the power gain in decibels, noise figure in decibels, and equivalent noise temperature for the whole amplifier.

SOLUTION

The power gain is the product of the individual gains:

$$A_T = A_1 A_2 A_3 = 10 \times 25 \times 30 = 7500 = 38.8 \text{ dB}$$

The noise figure is found from

$$NF_T = NF_1 + \frac{NF_2 - 1}{A_1} + \frac{NF_3 - 1}{A_1 A_2} + \cdots$$
$$= 2 + \frac{4 - 1}{10} + \frac{5 - 1}{10 \times 25}$$
$$= 2.316$$
$$= 3.65 \text{ dB}$$

The equivalent noise temperature is:

$$T_{eq} = 290(NF - 1)$$
$$= 290(2.316 - 1)$$
$$= 382 \text{ K}$$

1.16 TIME DOMAIN

An ordinary oscilloscope display, showing amplitude on one scale and time on the other, is a good example.

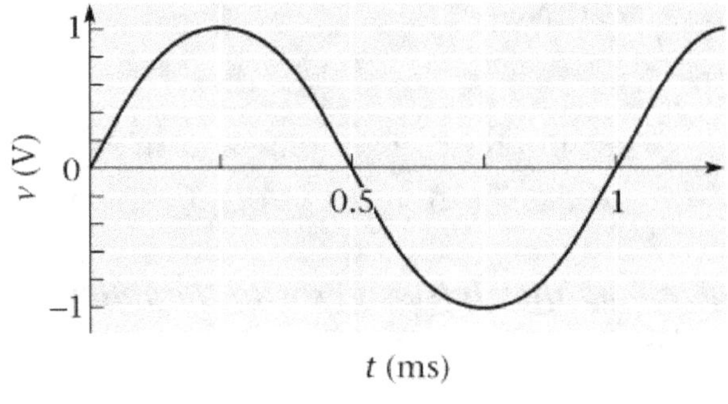

(a) Time domain

1.17 FREQUENCY DOMAIN

In a frequency domain representation, amplitude or power is shown on one axis and frequency is displayed on the other.

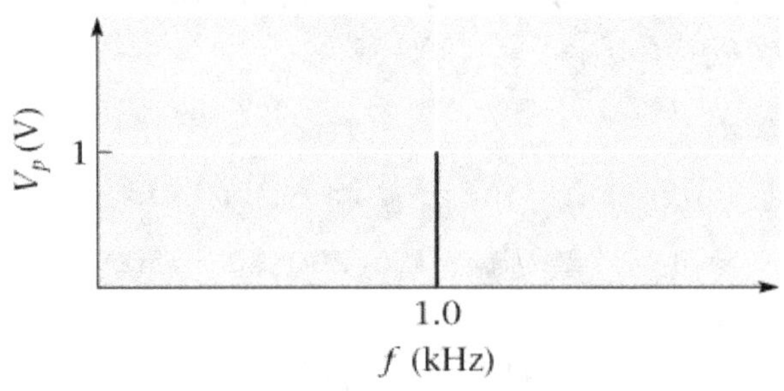

(b) Frequency domain

1.18 THE RADIO-FREQUENCY SPECTRUM

Radio waves are a form of electromagnetic radiation, as are infrared, visible light, ultraviolet light, and gamma rays. The major difference is in the frequency of the waves. The portion of the frequency spectrum that is useful for radio communication at present extends from roughly 100 kHz to about 50 GHz.

Frequency Designation	Frequency Range	Wavelength Range	Wavelength Designation
Extremely High Frequency (EHF)	30–300 GHz	1 mm–1 cm	Millimeter Waves
Super High Frequency (SHF)	3–30 GHz	1–10 cm	Microwaves (microwave region conventionally starts at 1 GHz)
Ultra High Frequency (UHF)	300 Mhz–3 GHz	10 cm–1 m	
Very High Frequency (VHF)	30–300 MHz	1–10 m	
High Frequency (HF)	3–30 MHz	10–100 m	Short Waves
Medium Frequency (MF)	300 kHz–3 MHz	100 m–1 km	Medium Waves

Table: Radio frequency spectrum

1.19 HARTLEY'S LAW

An unmodulated carrier would exist at only one frequency and has zero bandwidth. How much frequency range is needed for a carrier depends upon the baseband frequency range.

There is a general rule known as Hartley's Law which relates bandwidth, time, and information content. We will not yet be able to use it for actual calculations, but it would be well to note it for future reference, as Hartley's Law applies to the operation of all communication systems. Here it is:

$$I = ktB$$

where

I = amount of information to be transmitted in bits

k = a constant that depends on the modulation scheme and the signal-to-noise ratio

t = time in seconds

B = bandwidth in hertz

1.20 MULTIPLEXING

Multiplexing is a method by which multiple analog message signals or digital data streams are combined into one signal over a shared medium (Figure). The aim is to share an expensive resource. For example, several telephone calls may be carried using one wire.

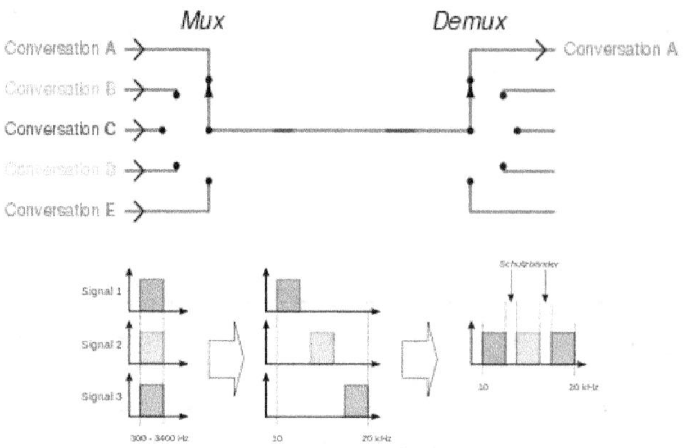

Fig: Multiplexing Techniques

1.21 Frequency Division Multiplexing (FDM)

When the available frequency range is divided among the signals, the process is known as frequency-division multiplexing (Figure). Radio and television signals are examples of FDM.

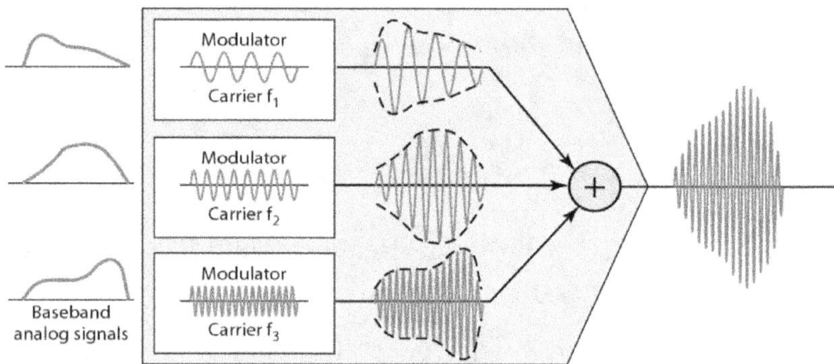

Fig: FDMA

Problem-1.3: *Five channels, each with a 100-kHz bandwidth, are to be multiplexed together. What is the minimum bandwidth of the link if there is a need for a guard band of 10 kHz between the channels to prevent interference?*

Solution:

For five channels, we need at least four guard bands. This means that the required bandwidth is at least

$5 \times 100 + 4 \times 10 = 540$ kHz

1.22 Time-Division Multiplexing (TDM)

Instead of dividing the bandwidth, the entire bandwidth is used for each signal, but only for a small part of the time. Digital telephone systems use TDM

1.23 FOURIER SERIES

Any well-behaved periodic waveform can be represented as a series of sine and/or cosine waves at multiples of its fundamental frequency (+ a dc offset). This is known as a Fourier series. Mathematically, a Fourier series is expressed by

$$f(t) = \frac{A_0}{2} + A_1 \cos \omega t + B_1 \sin \omega t + A_2 \cos 2\omega t + B_2 \sin 2\omega t + ...$$

A_n and B_n = real number coefficients

ω = fundamental frequency in radians per second

1.24 EFFECT OF FILTERING ON SIGNALS

Many signals have a bandwidth that is theoretically infinite. Limiting the frequency response of a channel removes some of these signals and causes the signal to be distorted. Shifting the phase angles of a square wave results in a signal other than a square wave. In general, the wider the bandwidth, the better the communication is.

1.25 WIRELESS COMMUNICATION

In radio transmission, it is necessary to send audio signal (e.g. music, speech etc.) from a broadcasting station over great distances to a receiver. This communication of audio signal does not employ any wire and is sometimes called wireless.

1.26 RADIO BROADCASTING, TRANSMISSION AND RECEPTION

Radio communication means the radiation of radio waves by the transmitting station, the propagation of these waves through space and their reception by the radio receiver. The entire arrangement can be divided into three parts viz. transmitter, transmission of radio waves and radio receiver.

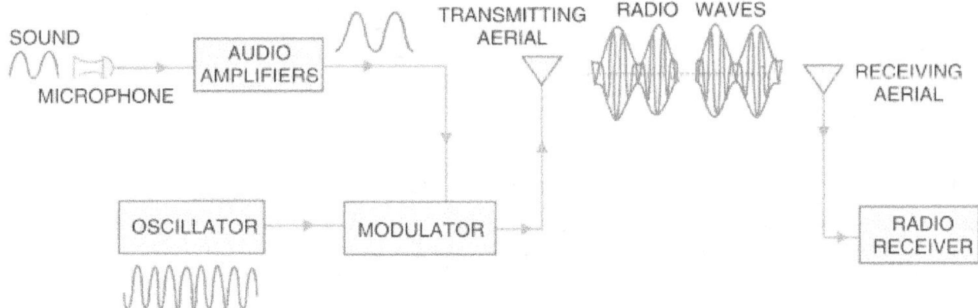

Fig: Radio Broadcasting, Transmission and Reception:

1. **Transmitter:**

Transmitter is an extremely important equipment and is housed in the broadcasting station. Its purpose is to produce radio waves for transmission into space. The important components of a transmitter are microphone, audio amplifiers, oscillator and modulator.

i. **Microphone:** A microphone is a device which converts sound waves into electrical waves. When the speaker speaks or a musical instrument is played, the varying air pressure on the microphone generates an audio electrical signal which corresponds in frequency to the original signal. The output of microphone is fed to a multistage audio amplifier for raising the strength of weak signal.

ii. **Audio amplifier:** The audio signal from the microphone is quite weak and requires amplification. This job is accomplished by cascaded audio amplifiers. The amplified output from the last audio amplifier is fed to the modulator for rendering the process of modulation.

iii. **Oscillator:** The function of oscillator is to produce a high frequency signal, called a carrier wave. Usually, a crystal oscillator is used for the purpose. The power level of the carrier wave is raised to a sufficient level by radio frequency amplifier stages. Most of the broadcasting stations have carrier wave power of several kilowatts. Such high power is necessary for transmitting the signal to the required distances.

iv. **Modulator:** The amplified audio signal and carrier wave are fed to the modulator. Here, the audio signal is superimposed on the carrier wave in a suitable manner. The resultant waves are called modulated waves or radio waves and the process is called modulation. The process of modulation permits the transmission of audio signal at the carrier frequency. As the carrier frequency is very high, therefore, the audio signal can be transmitted to large distances. The radio waves from the transmitter are fed to the transmitting antenna or aerial from where these are radiated into space.

2. Transmission of radio waves:

The transmitting antenna radiates the radio waves in space in all directions. These radio waves travel with the velocity of light i.e. 3×10^{8} m/sec. The radio waves are electromagnetic waves and possess the same general properties. These are similar to light and heat waves except that they have longer wavelengths. It may be emphasized here that radio waves are sent without employing any wire. It can be easily shown that at high frequency, electrical energy can be radiated into space.

3. Radio receiver:

On reaching the receiving antenna, the radio waves induce tiny e.m.f. in it. This small voltage is fed to the radio receiver. Here, the radio waves are first amplified and then signal is extracted from them by the process of demodulation. The signal is amplified by audio amplifiers and then fed to the speaker for reproduction into sound waves.

1.27 WHAT IS MODULATION?

The process of changing some characteristic (e.g. amplitude, frequency or phase) of a carrier wave in accordance with the intensity of the signal is known as modulation.

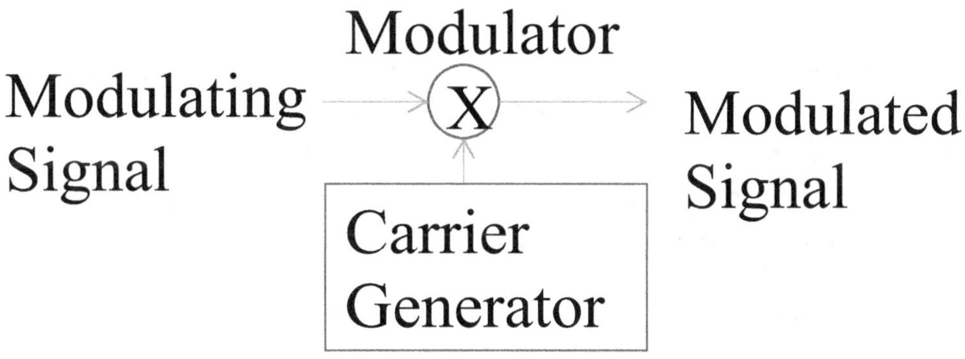

Fig: Modulation process

The baseband (information) signal is known as the modulating signal. The baseband signal is normally a low bandwidth signal. A periodic signal called the carrier is typically a high frequency sinusoidal wave. During the modulation process, the modulating signal varies the frequency, amplitude, or phase of the carrier in accordance with its instantaneous amplitude. The output of the modulator is called the modulated signal.

1.27.1 WHY MODULATION IS NEEDED?

Modulation is extremely necessary in communication system due to the following reasons:

i. **Practical antenna length:** Theory shows that in order to transmit a wave effectively, the length of the transmitting antenna should be approximately equal to the wavelength of the wave.

$$wavelength = \frac{velocity}{frequency} = \frac{3 \times 10^8}{frequency(Hz)} metres$$

As the audio frequencies range from 20 Hz to 20 kHz, therefore, if they are transmitted directly into space, the length of the transmitting antenna required would be extremely large. For instance, to radiate a frequency of 20 kHz directly into space, we would need an antenna length of $\frac{3 \times 10^8}{20 \times 10^3} = 15,000$ metres. This is too long antenna to be constructed practically. For this reason, it is impracticable to radiate audio signal directly into space. On the other hand, if a carrier wave say of 1000 kHz is used to carry the signal, we need an antenna length of 300 metres only and this size can be easily constructed.

ii. **Operating range:** The energy of a wave depends upon its frequency. The greater the frequency of the wave, the greater the energy possessed by it. As the audio signal frequencies are small, therefore, these cannot be transmitted over large distances if radiated directly into space. The only practical solution is to modulate a high frequency carrier wave with audio signal and permit the transmission to occur at this high frequency (i.e. carrier frequency).

iii. **Wireless communication:** One desirable feature of radio transmission is that it should be carried without wires i.e. radiated into space. At audio frequencies, radiation is not practicable because the efficiency of radiation is poor. However, efficient radiation of electrical energy is possible at high frequencies (> 20 kHz). For this reason, modulation is always done in communication systems.

1.27.2 Signals in the Modulation Process

Following are the three types of signals in the modulation process.

1. Message or Modulating Signal

The signal which contains a message to be transmitted, is called as a message signal. It is a baseband signal, which has to undergo the process of modulation, to get transmitted. Hence, it is also called as the modulating signal.

2. Carrier Signal

The high frequency signal, which has a certain amplitude, frequency and phase but contains no information is called as a carrier signal. It is an empty signal and is used to carry the signal to the receiver after modulation.

3. Modulated Signal

The resultant signal after the process of modulation is called as a modulated signal. This signal is a combination of modulating signal and carrier signal.

1.27.3 Types of Modulation

There are many types of modulations. Depending upon the modulation techniques used, they are classified as shown in the following figure.

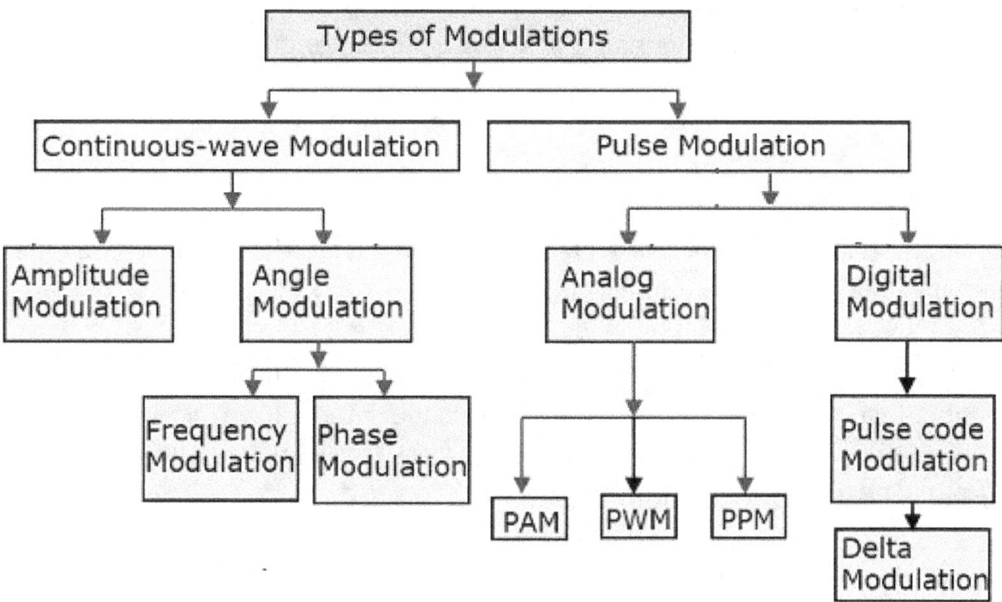

Fig: Types of Modulation

The types of modulations are broadly classified into continuous-wave modulation and pulse modulation.

1.27.4 CONTINUOUS-WAVE MODULATION

In continuous-wave modulation, a high frequency sine wave is used as a carrier wave. This is further divided into amplitude and angle modulation.

1. **Amplitude Modulation:**

If the amplitude of the high frequency carrier wave is varied in accordance with the instantaneous amplitude of the modulating signal, then such a technique is called as Amplitude Modulation.

2. **Angle Modulation:**

If the angle of the carrier wave is varied, in accordance with the instantaneous value of the modulating signal, then such a technique is called as Angle Modulation. Angle modulation is further divided into frequency modulation and phase modulation.

i. **Frequency Modulation:** If the frequency of the carrier wave is varied, in accordance with the instantaneous value of the modulating signal, then such a technique is called as Frequency Modulation.

ii.   **Phase Modulation:** If the phase of the high frequency carrier wave is varied in accordance with the instantaneous value of the modulating signal, then such a technique is called as Phase Modulation.

1.27.5 PULSE MODULATION

In Pulse modulation, a periodic sequence of rectangular pulses, is used as a carrier wave. This is further divided into analog and digital modulation.

In analog modulation technique, if the amplitude or duration or position of a pulse is varied in accordance with the instantaneous values of the baseband modulating signal, then such a technique is called as Pulse Amplitude Modulation (PAM) or Pulse Duration/Width Modulation (PDM/PWM), or Pulse Position Modulation (PPM).

In digital modulation, the modulation technique used is Pulse Code Modulation (PCM) where the analog signal is converted into digital form of 1s and 0s. As the resultant is a coded pulse train, this is called as PCM. This is further developed as Delta Modulation (DM). These digital modulation techniques are discussed in our Digital Communications tutorial

1.28 WHAT IS DEMODULATION?

The process of recovering the audio signal from the modulated wave is known as demodulation or detection.

At the broadcasting station, modulation is done to transmit the audio signal over larger distances to a receiver. When the modulated wave is picked up by the radio receiver, it is necessary to recover the audio signal from it. This process is accomplished in the radio receiver and is called demodulation.

1.28.1 WHY DEMODULATION IS NEEDED?

It was noted previously that amplitude modulated wave consists of carrier and sideband frequencies. The audio signal is contained in the sideband frequencies which are radio frequencies. If the modulated wave after amplification is directly fed to the speaker as shown in Fig, no sound will be heard. It is because diaphragm of the speaker is not at all able to respond to such high frequencies. Before the diaphragm is able to move in one direction, the rapid reversal of current tends to move it in the opposite direction i.e. diaphragm will not move at all. Consequently, no sound will be heard.

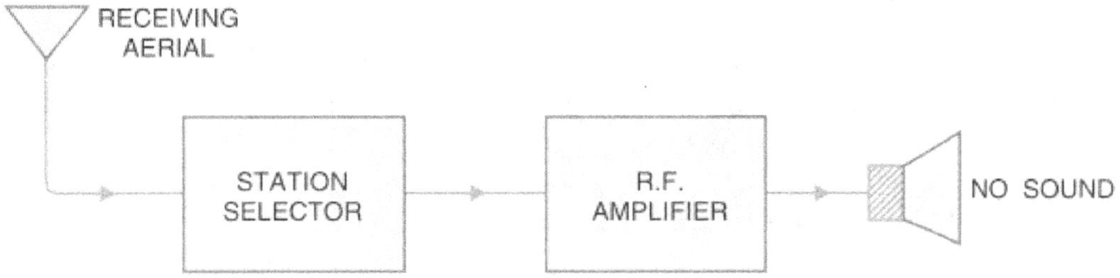

Fig: Receiver without demodulator

From the above discussion, it follows that audio signal must be separated from the carrier at a suitable stage in the receiver. The recovered audio signal is then amplified and fed to the speaker for conversion into sound.

1.28.2 FUNCTIONS OF DETECTOR CIRCUIT

It rectifies the modulated wave i.e. negative half of the modulated wave is eliminated. As shown in Fig(i), a modulated wave has positive and negative halves exactly equal. Therefore, average current is zero and speaker cannot respond. If the negative half of this modulated wave is eliminated as shown in Fig(ii), the average value of this wave will not be zero since the resultant pulses are now all in one direction. The average value is shown by the dotted line in Fig-14(ii).

Therefore, the diaphragm will have definite displacement corresponding to the average value of the wave. It may be seen that shape of the average wave is similar to that of the modulation envelope. As the signal is of the same shape as the envelope, therefore, average wave shape is of the same form as the signal.

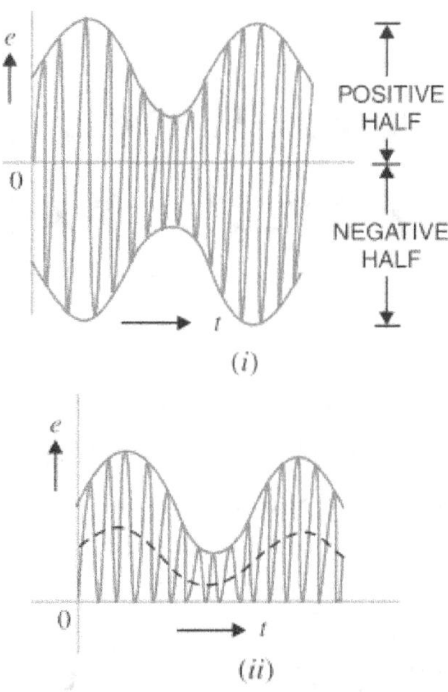

Fig: Functions of detector

It separates the audio signal from the carrier.

The rectified modulated wave contains the audio signal and the carrier. It is desired to recover the audio signal. This is achieved by a filter circuit which removes the carrier frequency and allows the audio signal to reach the load i.e. speaker.

1.29 Pre-emphasis and De-emphasis

Emphasis is the intentional alteration of the amplitude-vs.-frequency characteristics of the signal to reduce adverse effects of noise in a communication system. In processing electronic audio signals, pre-emphasis refers to a system process designed to increase (within a frequency band) the magnitude of some (usually higher) frequencies with respect to the magnitude of other (usually lower) frequencies.

A system process designed to decrease, (within a band of frequencies), the magnitude of some (usually higher) frequencies with respect to the magnitude of other (usually lower) frequencies is called De emphasis.

It improves the overall signal-to-noise ratio by minimizing the adverse effects of such phenomena as attenuation distortion or saturation of recording media in subsequent parts of the system.

Chapter-2

Radio Wave Propagation

2.1 Radio Waves

The electromagnetic waves in the frequency spectrum of 0.001 to 1000000 Hz are called to be radio waves. When a signal is transmitted from transmitter antenna, the radio wave which is actually radiated from antenna is spread in all directions. As the distance between transmitting antenna and receiving antenna is increased, the amplitude of Radio Wave is decreased.

2.2 What is Electromagnetic Wave Propagation?

Electromagnetic Waves also called Electromagnetic Radiations are basically defined as superimposed oscillations of an Electric and a Magnetic Field in space with their direction of propagation perpendicular to both of them.

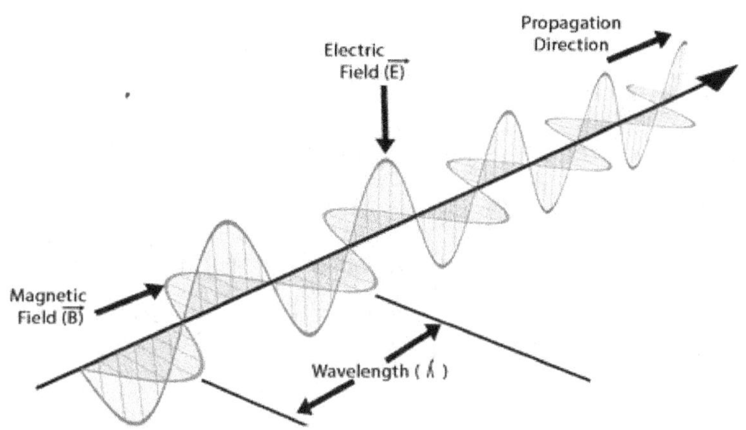

Fig: Electromagnetic wave propagation

Waves propagate through space as transverse electromagnetic (TEM) waves. This means that the electric field, the magnetic field, and the direction of travel of the wave are all mutually perpendicular.

2.2.1 PROPERTIES OF ELECTROMAGNETIC WAVE PROPAGATION

    i.   These waves travel at the speed of light.
   ii.   These waves do not require any medium for propagation.
  iii.   Electromagnetic waves travel in a transverse form.
  iv.   Electromagnetic waves are not deflected by electric or magnetic field.
   v.   These waves can be polarized.
  vi.   Electromagnetic Waves undergo interference and diffraction.

2.3 RADIO WAVES PROPAGATION EFFECTS

Propagation in free space and without any obstacle is the most ideal situation. When the radio waves reach close to an obstacle, the following propagation effects do occur to the waves:

1. Reflection:

Propagating wave impinges on an object that is larger as compared to its wavelength (for example, the surface of the earth, tall buildings, large walls).

2. Diffraction:

Radio path between a transmitter and a receiver is obstructed by a surface with sharp irregular edges (for example, waves bend around the obstacle, even when line of sight (LOS) does not exist).

3. Scattering:

When objects are smaller than the wavelength of the propagating wave (for example, foliage, street signs, lamp posts), incoming signal is scattered into several weaker outgoing signals.

Diffraction and scattering result in small-scale fading effects, while reflection results in a large-scale fading.

A typical propagation effect of mobile radio is shown in Figure. Here, h_b is the height of antenna from the earth's surface at the BS, h_m is the height of antenna from the earth's surface at the MS, and d is the distance between the BS and the MS.

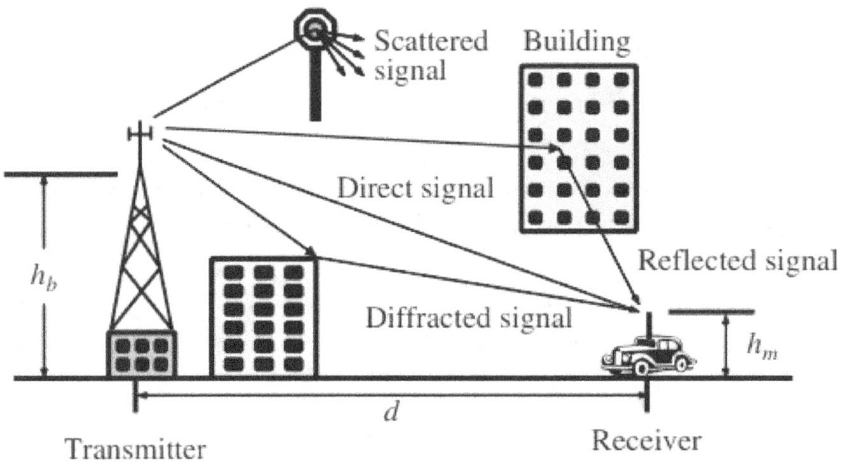

Fig: Reflection, diffraction, and scattering of radio signals.

The radio signals can penetrate simple walls, to some extent. However, a large street structure or hill is difficult to pass through. In those cases, diffracted and reflected radio waves enable the signals to reach these locations that are not directly in line with the direct path and help cover the neighborhood areas.

The disadvantage is that MSs may receive multiple copies of the same signals with appropriate delays corresponding to the traversed paths. The advances in signal processing take care of this problem by selecting the best quality of the received signal and filtering out the rest of the weaker copies or combining the multiple signals after compensating for their arrival phases. All these operations are done in the hand-set of the MS and are transparent to the user.

2.4 RADIO WAVES PROPAGATION MECHANISM

The method by which the Radio Waves travel in the free space is called Mode of Propagation. When an electromagnetic wave is sent out from an antenna, part of the radiated energy travels along or near the surface of the earth while the other part travels upward in space. The energy may reach the receiving antenna over any of the possible propagation modes which are as follows –

1. Free Space Propagation
2. Ground Wave Propagation
3. Sky Wave Propagation (Ionospheric Propagation)
4. Space Wave (Line of Sight) Propagation
5. Tropospheric Scatter Propagation
6. Duct Propagation

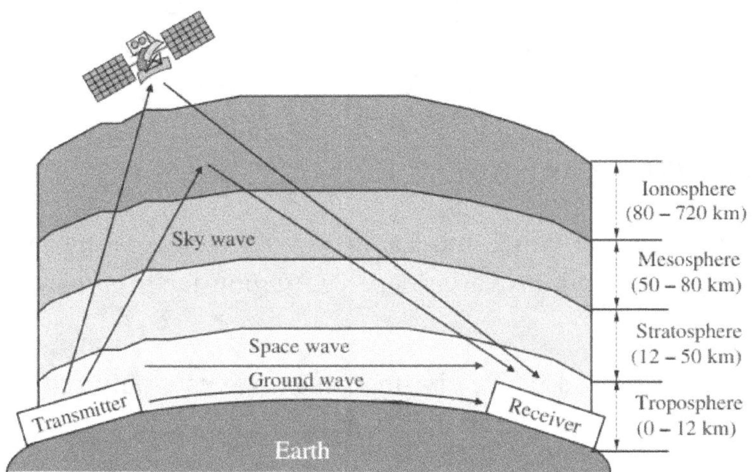

Fig: Propagation of different types of radio waves

	Modes of Propagation	Frequency Range
1	Ground Wave or Surface Wave Propagation	upto 2 MHz.
2	Sky Wave or Ionospheric Wave Propagation	between 2 to 30 MHz.
3	Tropospheric Scatter Propagation or Forward Scatter Propagation	UHF and microwaves above 300 MHz.
4	Space Wave or Line of Sight Propagation	above microwave range.
5	Duct Propagation	above microwave range.

As the name indicates, the ground wave propagates along the surface of the earth, and the sky wave propagates in the space but can return to earth by reflection either in the troposphere or in the ionosphere.

Based on the attributes of these waves, we can partition the spectrum. Classification of the radio spectrum is based on propagation properties and the system aspects. Table 1 shows the radio frequency bands used for radio transmission.

Classification Band	Initials	Frequency Range	Propagation Mode
Extremely low	ELF	<300 Hz ~3 kHz	Ground wave
Infra low	ILF	300 Hz ~3 kHz	Ground wave
Very low	VLF	3 kHz ~30 kHz	Ground wave
Low	LF	30 kHz ~300 kHz	Ground wave
Medium	MF	300 kHz ~3 MHz	Ground/sky wave
High	HF	3 MHz ~30 MHz	Sky wave
Very high	VHF	30 MHz ~300 MHz	Space wave
Ultra high	UHF	300 MHz ~3 GHz	Space wave
Super high	SHF	3 GHz ~30 GHz	Space wave
Extremely high	EHF	30 GHz ~300 GHz	Space wave
Tremendously high	THF	300 GHz ~3000 GHz	Space wave

Table: Radio Frequency Bands

2.4.1 FREE-SPACE PROPAGATION

As we know that in the surrounding environment in which the Radio Wave is propagating may have obstacles, discontinuities and propagation medium variations. The region far from earth's surface realized as a Free Space Propagation.

The simplest source of electromagnetic waves would be a point in space. Waves would radiate equally from this source in all directions. Such a source is called an isotropic radiator and is shown in Figure 4.

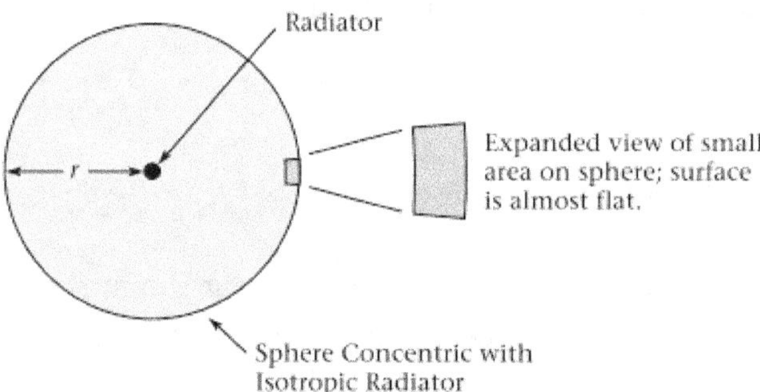

Fig: Isotropic radiator

Since an isotropic radiator radiates equally in all directions, the power density, in watts per square meter, is simply the total power divided by the surface area of the sphere. Put mathematically,

$$P_D = \frac{P_t}{4\pi r^2}$$

where

P_D = power density in W/m^2

P_t = transmitted power in W

r = distance from the antenna in meters

Real antennas do not radiate equally in all directions. If we define antenna gain as follows:

$$G_t = \frac{P_{DA}}{P_{DI}}$$

where

G_t = transmitting antenna gain

P_{DA} = power density in a given direction from the real antenna

P_{DI} = power density at the same distance from an isotropic radiator with the same P_t

Antennas are passive devices and do not have actual power gain. They achieve a greater power density in certain directions at the expense of reduced radiation in other directions. Now we can modify the power density equation to include antenna gain:

$$P_D = \frac{P_t G_t}{4\pi r^2}$$

Usually, antenna gain is specified in dBi. Where, the "i" indicates gain with respect to an isotropic radiator.

We can define the effective isotropic radiated power (EIRP) of a transmitting system in a given direction as the transmitter power that would be needed, with an isotropic radiator, to produce the same power density in the given direction. Therefore, it is apparent that

$$EIRP = P_t G_t$$

$$P_D = \frac{EIRP}{4\pi r^2}$$

2.4.1.1 Receiving Antenna Gain and Effective Area:

A receiving antenna absorbs some of the energy from radio waves that pass it. Since the power in the wave is proportional to the area through which it passes, a large antenna will intercept more energy than a smaller one (other things being equal) because it intercepts a larger area. Antennas are also more efficient at absorbing power from some directions than from others.

For instance, a satellite dish would not be very efficient if it were pointed at the ground instead of the satellite. In other words, receiving antennas have gain, just as transmitting antennas do. In fact, the gain is the same whether the antenna is used for receiving or transmitting.

The power extracted from the wave by a receiving antenna depends both on its physical size and on its gain. The effective area of an antenna can be defined as

$$A_{eff} = \frac{P_r}{P_D}$$

where

A_{eff} = effective area of the antenna in m^2
P_r = power delivered to the receiver in W
P_D = power density of the wave in W/m^2

The effective area of an antenna is the area from which all the power in the wave is extracted and delivered to the receiver. Combining Equation

$$P_r = A_{eff}P_D$$

$$= \frac{A_{eff}P_tG_t}{4\pi r^2}$$

It can be shown that the effective area of a receiving antenna is

$$A_{eff} = \frac{\lambda^2 G_r}{4\pi}$$

where

G_r = antenna gain, as a power ratio
λ = wavelength of the signal

Problem-2.1: A power of 100 W is supplied to an isotropic radiator. What is the power density at a point 10 km away?

$$P_D = \frac{P_t}{4\pi r^2}$$

$$= \frac{100 \text{ W}}{4\pi(10 \times 10^3 \text{ m})^2}$$

$$= 79.6 \text{ nW/m}^2$$

Problem-2.2: The transmitter of Problem 1 is used with an antenna having a gain of 5 dBi. Calculate the EIRP and the power density at a distance of 10 km.

First convert the gain to a power ratio.

$$G_t = \log^{-1}\left(\frac{5}{10}\right)$$

$$= 3.16$$

This means that the EIRP in the given direction is about three times the actual transmitter power. More precisely,

$$EIRP = G_t P_t = 3.16 \times 100 \text{ W} = 316 \text{ W}$$

The power density is

$$P_D = \frac{EIRP}{4\pi r^2}$$

$$= \frac{316}{4\pi(10 \times 10^3)^2}$$

$$= 251.5 \text{ nW/m}^2$$

2.4.1.2 Path Loss:

The receiver power in terms of antenna gain

$$P_r = \frac{A_{eff} P_t G_t}{4\pi r^2}$$

$$= \frac{\lambda^2 G_r P_t G_t}{(4\pi)(4\pi r^2)}$$

$$= \frac{\lambda^2 P_t G_t G_r}{16\pi^2 r^2}$$

$$P_r = P_t + G_t + G_r - (32.44 + 20 \log d + 20 \log f)$$

where

P_r = received power in dBm
P_t = transmitted power in dBm
G_t = transmitting antenna gain in dBi
G_r = receiving antenna gain in dBi
d = distance between transmitter and receiver, in km
f = frequency in MHz

$$P_r = P_t + G_t + G_r - L_{fs}$$

$$L_{fs} = 32.44 + 20 \log d + 20 \log f$$

where

L_{fs} = free-space loss in decibels

Equation shows the free space path loss characteristics as a function of the transmitting frequency and the distance of the receiver from the transmitter. It is clear from the figure 5 that the signal strength reduced with the distance and the path loss also increases with the carrier frequency.

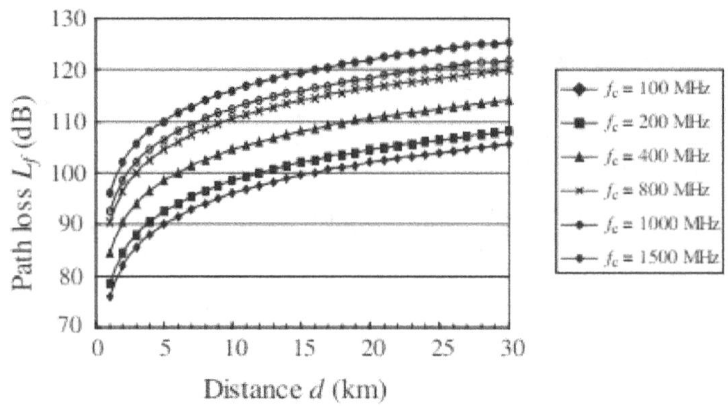

Fig: Free space path loss

Problem-2.3: A transmitter has a power output of 150 W at a carrier frequency of 325 MHz. It is connected to an antenna with a gain of 12 dBi. The receiving antenna is 10 km away and has a gain of 5 dBi. Calculate the power delivered to the receiver, assuming free-space propagation. Assume also that there are no losses or mismatches in the system.

<u>SOLUTION</u>

In all problems of this sort, it is a good idea to begin by sketching the system. This example can be done easily enough without such a sketch, but many real-world situations are more complex. See Figure for the setup.

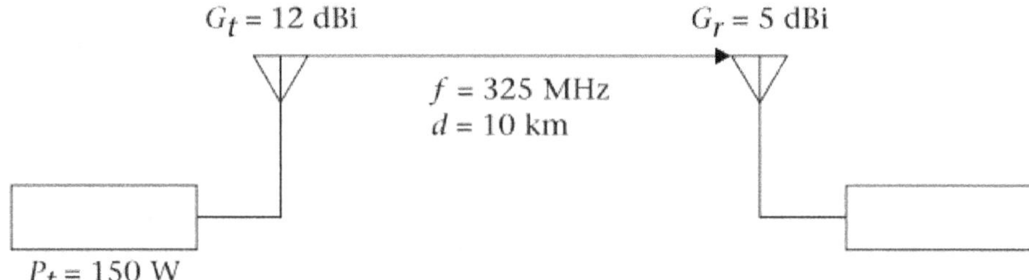

The next step is to convert the transmitter power into dBm:

$$P_t(\text{dBm}) = 10\log\left(\frac{P_t}{1\,\text{mW}}\right)$$

$$= 10\log\left(\frac{150\,\text{W}}{0.001\,\text{W}}\right)$$

$$= 51.8\ \text{dBm}$$

Marking the transmitter power and antenna gains on the sketch shows us that the only missing link is the path loss.

$$\begin{aligned}
L_{fs} &= 32.44 + 20 \log d + 20 \log f \\
&= 32.44 + 20 \log 10 + 20 \log 325 \\
&= 102.7 \text{ dB}
\end{aligned}$$

Now we can easily find the received power

$$\begin{aligned}
P_r &= P_t + G_t + G_r - L_{fs} \\
&= 51.8 + 12 + 5 - 102.7 \\
&= -33.9 \text{ dBm}
\end{aligned}$$

***Problem-2.4:** A taxi company uses a central dispatcher, with an antenna at the top of a 15 m tower, to communicate with taxicabs. The taxi antennas are on the roofs of the cars, approximately 1.5 m above the ground. Calculate the maximum communication distance:*

I. between the dispatcher and a taxi

II. between two taxis

SOLUTION

$$\text{(a)} \qquad d = \sqrt{17h_t} + \sqrt{17h_r}$$

$$= \sqrt{17 \times 15} + \sqrt{17 \times 1.5}$$

$$= 21 \text{ km}$$

$$\text{(b)} \qquad d = \sqrt{17h_t} + \sqrt{17h_r}$$

$$= \sqrt{17 \times 1.5} + \sqrt{17 \times 1.5}$$

$$= 10.1 \text{ km}$$

2.4.2 GROUND (SURFACE) WAVES PROPAGATION

Ground Wave propagation is a method of radio wave propagation that uses the area between the surface of the earth and the ionosphere for transmission. The ground wave can propagate a considerable distance over the earth's surface particularly in the low frequency and medium frequency portion of the radio spectrum.

Ground waves progress along the surface of the earth and must be vertically polarized to prevent short circuiting the electric component. A wave induces currents in the ground over which it passes and thus loses some energy by absorption. This is made up by energy diffracted downward from the upper portions of the wave front.

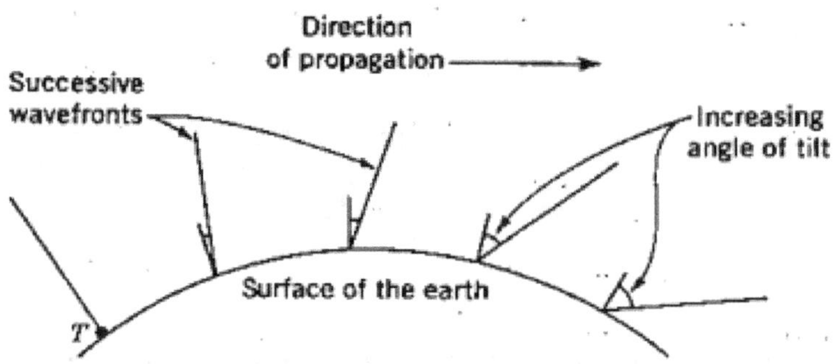

Fig: Ground wave propagation

There is another way in which the surface wave is attenuated: because of diffraction, the wave front gradually tilts over, as shown in Figure. As the wave propagates over the earth, it tilts over more and more, and the increasing tilt causes greater short circuiting of the electric field component of the wave and hence field strength reduction.

Eventually, at some distance (in wavelengths) from the antenna over which the ground wave propagates, the wave "lies down and dies." It is important to realize this, since it shows that the maximum range of such a transmitter depends on its frequency as well as its power. Thus, in the VLF band, insufficient range of transmission can be cured by increasing the transmitting power.

Radiation from an antenna by means of the ground wave gives rise to a field strength at a distance, which may be calculated by use of Maxwell's equations. This field strength, in volts per meter, is given by

$$\mathscr{E} = \frac{120\pi h_t\, I}{\lambda d}$$

If a receiving antenna is now placed at this point, the signal it will receive will be; in volts,

$$V = \frac{120\pi h_t\, h_r\, I}{\lambda d}$$

where 120π = characteristic impedance of free space

h_t = effective height (this is not quite the same as the actual height, for reasons dealt with in Section 9-4) of the transmitting antenna

h_r = effective height of the receiving antenna

I = antenna current

d = distance from the transmitting antenna

λ = wavelength

Ground wave is used for a low-frequency range transmission, mostly less than 1 MHz. This type of propagation employs the use of large antennas order of which is equivalent to the wavelength of the waves and uses the ground or Troposphere for its propagation. Signals over large distances are not sent using this method. It causes severe attenuation which increases with increased frequency of the waves.

The attenuation of surface waves increases very rapidly with increase in frequency, hence ground wave propagation is used for low frequency and large wavelength i.e. AM waves.

The range of frequency is from a few KHz to few MHz (5 MHz).

Advantages

As the ground wave propagation support large wavelength, the wave can bend round the corners/obstructions more efficiently.

Disadvantages

- Ground wave propagation can only be used for short range.
- As it is amplitude modulated, it gathers noise while transmission.
- As the frequency range is also small only a limited number of transmitters can be used.

As ground wave propagation works with low frequency range and short distance, so it is not suitable for radio signal transmission hence, the use of ground wave propagation is very limited.

A ground wave mobile radio channel is characterized by communication from/to a fixed station to/from a MS; it becomes a multipath propagation channel with fading.

The received signal power P_r is expressed as

$$P_r = \frac{G_t G_r P_t}{L}.$$

Where, L represents the propagation loss in the channel. Wave propagation in a mobile radio channel is characterized by three aspects: path loss, slow fading (shadowing), and fast fading. Therefore, L can be expressed as

$$L = L_P L_S L_F.$$

Where, L_P, L_S, and L_F represent the path loss, slow fading loss, and fast fading

2.4.2.1 Path Loss:

The path loss L_P is the average propagation loss over a wide area. It is determined by the macroscopic parameters, such as the distance between the transmitter and receiver, the carrier frequency, and the land profile loss, respectively.

$$L_f (\text{dB}) = 32.45 + 20 \log_{10} f_c \text{ (MHz)} + 20 \log_{10} d \text{ (km)}.$$

2.4.2.2 Fading:

Fading refers to variation in signal strength with respect to time as it is received at the antenna from the transmitter at distant end. The variation can be result of communication channel between the transmitter and receiver.

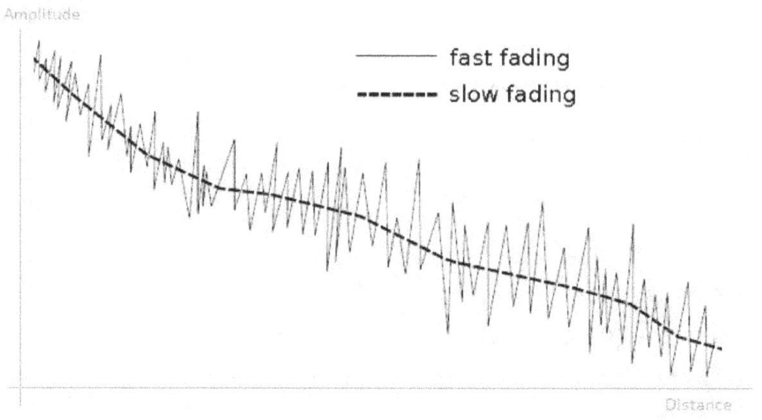

Fig: Fast and Slow fading

2.4.2.2.1 Slow Fading:

Slow fading is caused by movement over distances large enough to produce gross variations in overall path length between base station and mobile station. In other words, the long term variation in the mean level is known as slow fading.

- Does not vary quickly with the frequency
- Changes signal path due to obstructions and shadowing
- Low Doppler speed
- Impulse response changes much slower
- Coherence time>>symbol period

2.4.2.2.2 Fast Fading:

Rapid fluctuations caused by local multipath are known as fast fading. It is short-term fading.

- Varies quickly with frequency
- Originates due to constructive and destructive interference
- High Doppler speed
- Channel impulse response changes rapidly within the symbol duration
- Coherence time << symbol period

2.4.3   SKY-WAVE PROPAGATION

Radio Waves in lower frequencies and middle frequencies ranges may also propagate as ground waves but suffer significant losses or are attenuated particularly at higher frequencies. But as the ground wave mode fades out, a new mode developed known as the Sky Wave. These waves are reflected back from the ionosphere.

The electromagnetic waves emitted by transmitting antenna are received after being reflected from the ionosphere are called sky waves and this type propagation is called Sky wave Propagation. The sky waves are the radio waves of frequency between 2 MHz to 30 MHz. These radio waves can propagate through atmosphere and are reflected back by the ionosphere of earth's atmosphere.

The sky waves are of practical importance at medium and high frequencies (i.e. at medium waves and short waves) for very long distance radio communication. The sky wave propagation is also known as ionosphere propagation, since the sky waves reach the receiver after reflection from the ionosphere.

In a single reflection from the ionosphere, the radio waves cover a distance not more than 4000 km. With the help of sky wave propagation, a very long distance round the globe communication is possible.

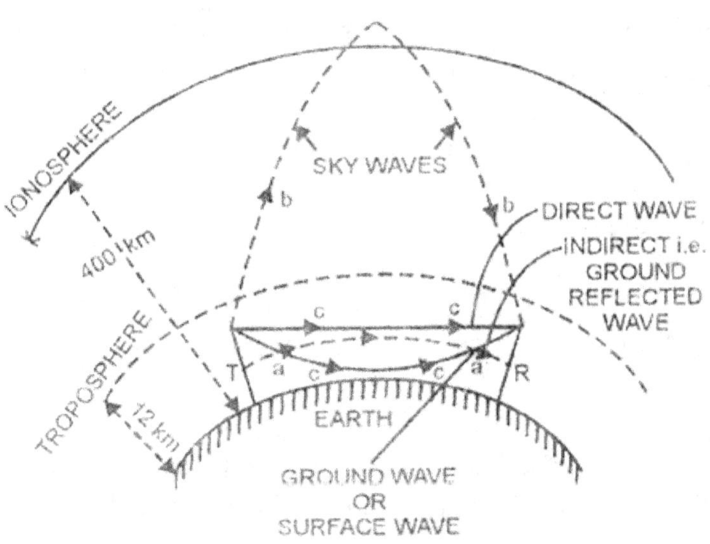

Fig: Sky wave propagation

The simplest manifestation of polarization to visualize is that of a plane wave, which is a good approximation of most light waves.

Polarization is basically classified in three ways:

- ➢ Linear Polarization
- ➢ Circular Polarization
- ➢ Elliptical Polarization

Sky wave is used for the propagation of EM waves with a frequency range of 3 – 30 MHz. Make use of the ionosphere so called due to the presence of charged ions in the region of about 60 to 300 km from the earth surface. These ions provide a reflecting medium to the radio or communication waves within a particular frequency range. We use this property of the ionosphere for long-distance transmission of the waves without much attenuation and loss of signal strength.

The frequency range for sky wave propagation is from 3 MHz to 32 MHz. The phenomenon responsible for sky wave propagation is reflection due to ionosphere and the type of reflection is total internal reflection.

Advantages

Sky wave propagation can be used for long distance communication.

2.4.4   SPACE WAVE PROPAGATION

The high frequency electromagnetic wave is not reflected back by the ionosphere, so to use high frequency electromagnetic wave in communication we used space wave propagation.

Space waves are used in two types of communication –

- i.   Line-of-sight (LOS) propagation.
- ii.   Satellite communication

2.4.1 LINE-OF-SIGHT (LOS) PROPAGATION

In line of sight propagation a space wave travels in a straight line from transmitting antenna to the receiving antenna at frequencies below 40 MHz. For this type of propagation there should be no obstacle between the transmitting antenna and the receiving antenna.

In order for this to occur, the two antennas must be able to see e ach other i.e. there must be a Line of Sight path between them. The practical communication distance for line-of-sight propagation is limited by the curvature of the earth.

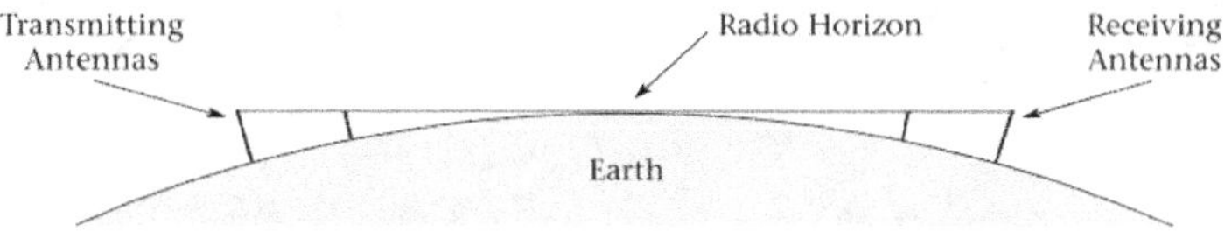

Fig: Line-of-sight propagation

In line-of-sight propagation, space waves are very powerful, the signals are very clear, the bandwidth is very large and a huge amount of information can be transmitted.

There is a very important relationship for determining the height of the antennas and their corresponding distance of transmission given by:

$$d = \sqrt{17h_t} + \sqrt{17h_r}$$

where

d = maximum distance in kilometers

h_t = height of the transmitting antenna in meters

h_r = height of the receiving antenna in meters

2.4.2 SATELLITE COMMUNICATION

For a frequency more than 40 MHz, ground wave propagation and sky wave propagation cannot be used. So this high frequency signals are transmitted at a particular angle from the surface of the earth towards the satellite. After hitting the satellite the signal wave is reflected back if the satellite is an inert satellite but the reflected wave is very weak so it is not possible to receive it back. Instead of inert satellite, active satellite is used for satellite communication.

Active satellite should have the following characteristics −

- It should be a geo-stationary satellite.
- The satellite has a repeater system i.e. it includes a receiver, amplifier, transmitter.

In satellite communication the process of transmitting signal wave towards the satellite is known as uplinking. The satellite has a receiver that receives the incoming message signal and then amplifies the signal and the frequency of the signal is also changed, after which the message signal is transmitted back to the earth. This type of propagation is known as space wave propagation and as satellite is used the communication is called as satellite communication.

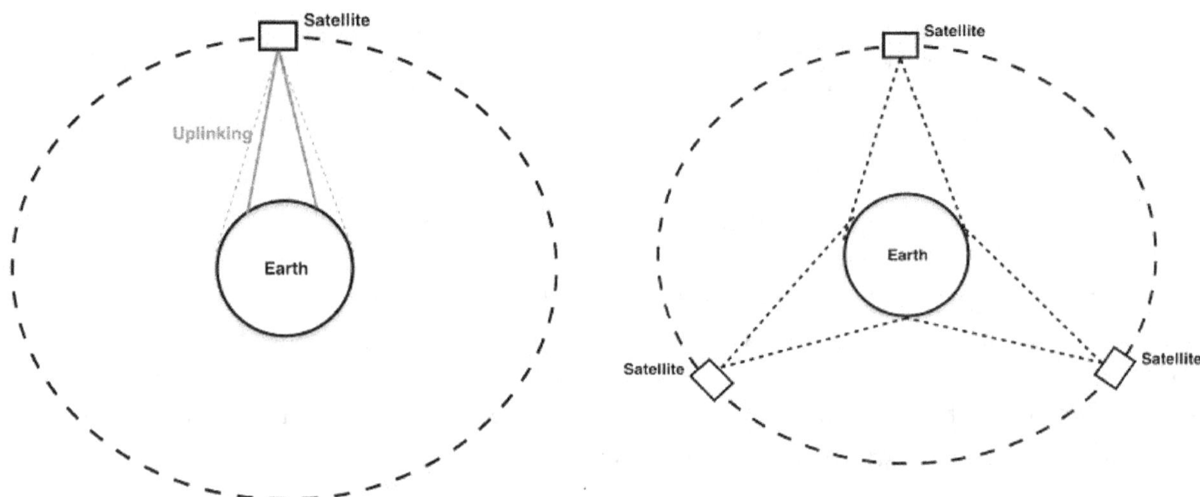

Fig: Satellite Communication

The range for receiving the signal transmitted form the satellite is more than 1/3rd of the earth.

If it is required that the message signal should reach to a distance larger than the range of the satellite, then global communication system is used which is a combination of three different satellites.

When the message signal is to be transmitted beyond the range of a satellite that particular satellite sends the message signal to another satellite via a special frequency and the message signal is delivered.

Space wave is used for a line of Sight communication also known as LOS. Space satellite communication and very high-frequency waves use this propagation method. It basically involves sending a signal in a straight line from the transmitter to the receiver. We must ensure that for very large distances, the height of the tower used for transmission is high enough to prevent waves from touching the earth curvature thus preventing attenuation and loss of signal strength.

Effect of various parameters on Space Wave Propagation:

    a. Curvature of the earth
    b. Effect of earth's imperfections
    c. Effect of hills, buildings
    d. Effect of polarization and transition between ground wave and space waves

2.4.5 TROPOSPHERIC SCATTER PROPAGATION

The technique is of practical importance at VHF, UHF and Microwaves. The UHF and Microwave Signals are found to be propagated much beyond to the Line of Sight Propagation through the forward scattering in the tropospheric irregularities. The Mode of Propagation which uses properties of scattering in Troposphere is known as Tropospheric Scatter Propagation. Here comes a term, the method for improving the reliability of troposcatter links is known as Diversity Operations.

Advantages of Tropospheric Scatter/Diffraction –

  i.   Provides reliable multichannel communication.
  ii. Reduces number of station required to cover a given large distance when compared to radio links.
  iii. It is best suited to meet tall connecting requirements of areas of population density.
  iv. It can be used in thin line military systems with links upto 1480 kms.
  v.   Desirable for multichannel communication.
  vi. Requires less maintenance staff per route kilometre than conventional line of sight microwave systems over the same route.

Disadvantages of Tropospheric Scatter/Diffraction –

  i.   It typically displays larger losses then Radio Link Path.
  ii. More financial investment are laid in the installation of Tropospheric Scatter phenomena in comparison to the
  iii. LOS Microwave installation.

2.4.6 DUCT PROPAGATION

The special refraction of electromagnetic waves is called Super Refraction and the process is called Duct Propagation. Duct is mainly formed by the temperature inversion. A duct is formed between the two such layer in which the electromagnetic wave guided as in a Wave Guide.

CHAPTER-3
AMPLITUDE MODULATION

3.1 AMPLITUDE MODULATION

When the amplitude of high frequency carrier wave is changed in accordance with the intensity of the signal, it is called amplitude modulation.

In amplitude modulation, only the amplitude of the carrier wave is changed in accordance with the intensity of the signal. However, the frequency of the modulated wave remains the same i.e. carrier frequency. Fig shows the principle of amplitude modulation.

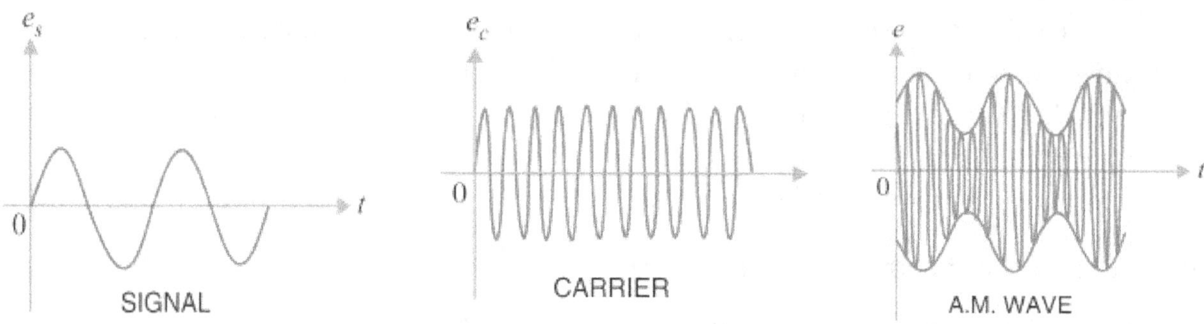

Fig: Amplitude Modulation

Note that the amplitudes of both positive and negative half-cycles of carrier wave are changed in accordance with the signal. Amplitude modulation is done by an electronic circuit called modulator.

The following points are worth noting in amplitude modulation:

> The amplitude of the carrier wave changes according to the intensity of the signal.
> The amplitude variations of the carrier wave is at the signal frequency f_s.
> The frequency of the amplitude modulated wave remains the same i.e. carrier frequency f_c.

3.1.1 ENVELOPE

The imaginary pattern formed by connecting the peaks of individual RF waveforms in AM signal.

3.1.2 MODULATION INDEX (M)

The ratio of change of amplitude of carrier wave to the amplitude of normal carrier wave is called the modulation index m i.e.

$$Modulation\ index,\ m = \frac{Amplitude\ change\ of\ carrier\ wave}{Normal\ carrier\ amplitude\,(unmodulated)}$$

The value of modulation factor depends upon the amplitudes of carrier and signal.

(i) When signal amplitude is zero, the carrier wave is not modulated as shown in Fig. The amplitude of carrier wave remains unchanged.

$$Amplitude\ change\ of\ carrier\ =\ 0$$
$$Amplitude\ of\ normal\ carrier\ =\ A$$
$$Modulation\ factor,\ m\ =\ 0/A\ =\ 0\ or\ 0\%$$

Fig: When signal amplitude is zero

(ii) When signal amplitude is equal to the carrier amplitude as shown in Fig, the amplitude of carrier varies between 2A and zero.

$$Amplitude\ change\ of\ carrier\ =\ 2A - A\ =\ A$$
$$Modulation\ factor,\ m\ =\ \frac{Amplitude\ change\ of\ carrier}{Amplitude\ of\ normal\ carrier}\ =\ A/A\ =\ 1\ or\ 100\%$$

In this case, the carrier is said to be 100% modulated

Fig: When signal amplitude is equal to the carrier amplitude

(iii) When the signal amplitude is one-half the carrier amplitude as shown in Fig, the amplitude of carrier wave varies between 1.5 A and 0.5 A.

$$Amplitude\ change\ of\ carrier\ =\ 1.5\,A - A\ =\ 0.5\,A$$
$$Modulation\ factor,\ m\ =\ 0.5\,A/A\ =\ 0.5\ or\ 50\%$$

In this case, the carrier is said to be 50% modulated.

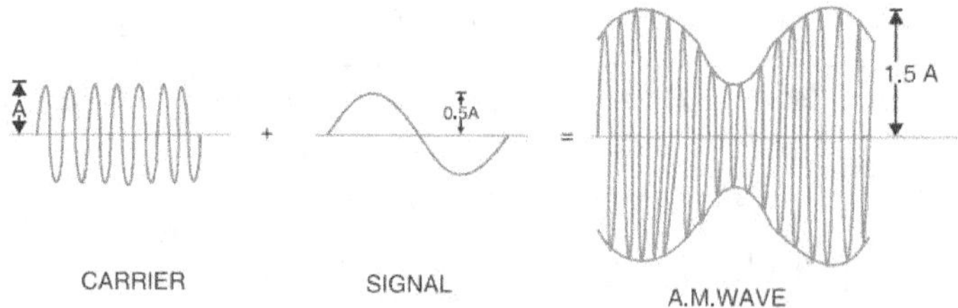

Fig: When signal amplitude is one-half the carrier amplitude

(iv)   When the signal amplitude is 1.5 times the carrier amplitude as shown in Fig, the maximum value of carrier wave becomes 2.5 A.

Amplitude change of carrier wave = 2.5 A − A= 1.5 A

Modulation factor,
$$m = \frac{1.5A}{A} = 1.5 = 150\%$$

In this case, the carrier is said to be 150% modulated i.e. over-modulated.

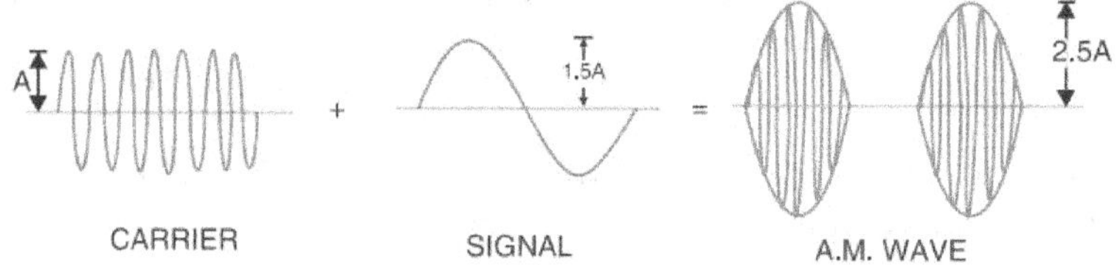

Fig: When signal amplitude is 1.5 times the carrier amplitude

MODULATION INDEX FOR MULTIPLE MODULATING FREQUENCIES

Two or more sine waves of different, uncorrelated frequencies modulating a single carrier is calculated by the equation:

$$m = \sqrt{m_1^2 + m_2^2 + \bullet\bullet\bullet}$$

Problem-3.1: Find the modulation index if a 10-volt carrier is amplitude modulated by three different frequencies, with amplitudes of 1, 2, and 3 volts respectively.

SOLUTION

The three separate modulation indices are:

$$m_1 = 1/10 = 0.1$$
$$m_2 = 2/10 = 0.2$$
$$m_3 = 3/10 = 0.3$$

$$
\begin{aligned}
m_T &= \sqrt{m_1^2 + m_2^2 + m_3^2} \\
&= \sqrt{0.1^2 + 0.2^2 + 0.3^2} \\
&= 0.374
\end{aligned}
$$

3.1.2.1 IMPORTANCE OF MODULATION INDEX

Modulation index is very important since it determines the strength and quality of the transmitted signal.

In an AM wave, the signal is contained in the variations of the carrier amplitude. When the carrier is modulated to a small degree (i.e. small m), the amount of carrier amplitude variation is small. Consequently, the audio signal being transmitted will not be very strong. The greater the degree of modulation (i.e. m), the stronger and clearer will be the audio signal.

It may be emphasised here that if the carrier is overmodulated (i.e. m> 1), distortion will occur during reception. This condition is shown in figure 5. The AM waveform is clipped and the envelope is discontinuous. Therefore, degree of modulation should never exceed 100%.

Problem-3.2: If the maximum and minimum voltages of an AM wave are V_{max} and V_{min} respectively, then show that modulation factor m is given by:

$$m = \frac{V_{max} - V_{min}}{V_{max} + V_{min}}$$

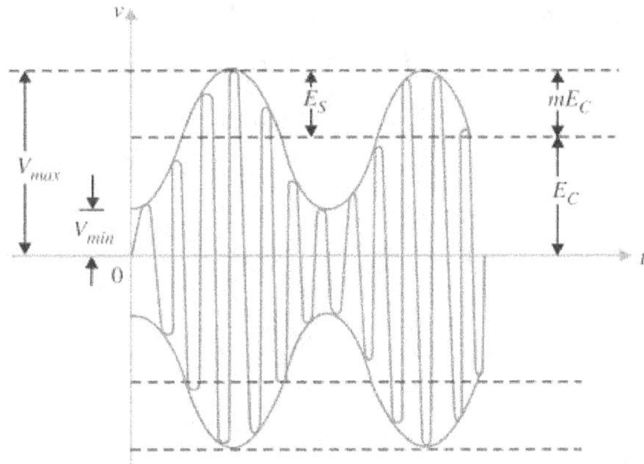

Let V_{max} and V_{min} be the maximum and minimum amplitudes of the modulated wave.

We will get the maximum amplitude of the modulated wave, when $\cos(2\pi f_m t)$ is 1.

$$\Rightarrow V_{max} = V_c + V_m$$

We will get the minimum amplitude of the modulated wave, when $\cos(2\pi f_m t)$ is -1.

$$\Rightarrow V_{min} = V_c - V_m$$

Add Equations

$$V_{max} + V_{min} = V_c + V_m + V_c - V_m = 2V_c$$

Let the amplitude of the normal carrier wave be E_c

$$E_C = \frac{V_{max} + V_{min}}{2}$$

If E_S is the signal amplitude

$$E_S = \frac{V_{max} - V_{min}}{2}$$

$$E_S = m\, E_C$$

$$\frac{V_{max} - V_{min}}{2} = m\,\frac{V_{max} + V_{min}}{2} \quad \text{or} \quad m = \frac{V_{max} - V_{min}}{V_{max} + V_{min}}$$

Problem-3.3: The maximum peak-to-peak voltage of an AM wave is 16 mV and the minimum peak-to-peak voltage is 4 mV. Calculate the modulation factor.

Solution.

Maximum voltage of AM wave is

$$V_{max} = \frac{16}{2} = 8\ \text{mV}$$

Minimum voltage of AM wave is

$$V_{min} = \frac{4}{2} = 2\ \text{mV}$$

$\therefore$ Modulation factor, $m = \dfrac{V_{max} - V_{min}}{V_{max} + V_{min}}$

$$= \frac{8-2}{8+2} = \frac{6}{10} = 0.6$$

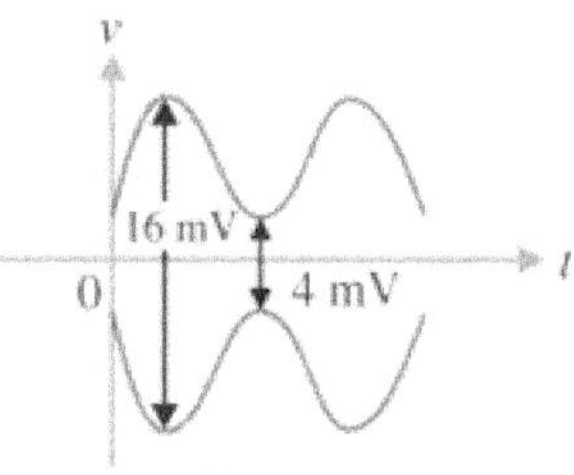

Problem-3.4: A carrier of 100V and 1200 kHz is modulated by a 50 V, 1000 Hz sine wave signal. Find the modulation factor.

Solution.

$$\text{Modulation factor, } m = \frac{E_S}{E_C} = \frac{50\ \text{V}}{100\ \text{V}} = 0.5$$

3.1.3 AM ANALYSIS

A carrier wave may be represented by :

$$e_c = E_C \cos \omega_c t$$

where e_c = instantaneous voltage of carrier

E_C = amplitude of carrier

ω_c = $2\pi f_c$

= angular velocity at carrier frequency f_c

In amplitude modulation, the amplitude E_C of the carrier wave is varied in accordance with the intensity of the signal as shown in Fig. 16.6. Suppose the modulation factor is m. It means that signal produces a maximum change of $m\,E_C$ in the carrier amplitude. Obviously, the amplitude of signal is $m\,E_C$. Therefore, the signal can be represented by :

$$e_s = m\,E_C \cos \omega_s t$$

where e_s = instantaneous voltage of signal

$m\,E_C$ = amplitude of signal

ω_s = $2\pi f_s$ = angular velocity at signal frequency f_s

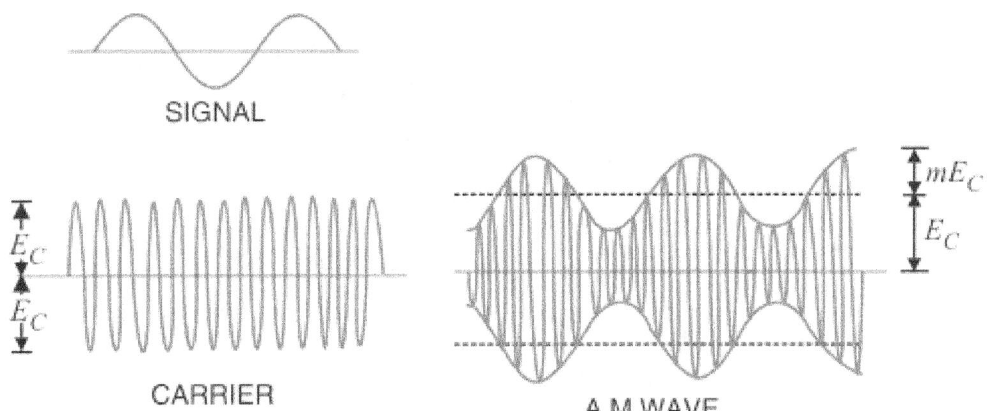

Fig: AM Modulation

The amplitude of the carrier wave varies at signal frequency f_s. Therefore, the amplitude of AM wave is given by :

$$\text{Amplitude of AM wave} = E_C + m\,E_C \cos \omega_s t = E_C (1 + m \cos \omega_s t)$$

The instantaneous voltage of AM wave is :

$$e = \text{Amplitude} \times \cos \omega_c t$$

$$= E_C (1 + m \cos \omega_s t) \cos \omega_c t$$

$$= E_C \cos \omega_c t + m\,E_C \cos \omega_s t \cos \omega_c t$$

$$= E_C \cos \omega_c t + \frac{mE_C}{2} (2 \cos \omega_s t \cos \omega_c t)$$

$$= E_C \cos \omega_c t + \frac{mE_C}{2} [\cos (\omega_c + \omega_s) t + \cos (\omega_c - \omega_s) t]^*$$

$$= E_C \cos \omega_c t + \frac{mE_C}{2} \cos (\omega_c + \omega_s) t + \frac{mE_C}{2} \cos (\omega_c - \omega_s) t$$

The following points may be noted from the above equation of amplitude modulated wave:

(*i*) The AM wave is equivalent to the summation of three sinusoidal waves; one having amplitude E_C and frequency **f_c, the second having amplitude $mE_c/2$ and frequency $(f_c + f_s)$ and the third having amplitude $mE_c/2$ and frequency $f_c - f_s$.

(*ii*) The AM wave contains three frequencies *viz* f_c, $f_c + f_s$ and $f_c - f_s$. The first frequency is the carrier frequency. Thus, the process of modulation does not change the original carrier frequency but produces two new frequencies $(f_c + f_s)$ and $(f_c - f_s)$ which are called sideband frequencies.

(*iii*) The sum of carrier frequency and signal frequency *i.e.* $(f_c + f_s)$ is called *upper sideband frequency*. The *lower sideband frequency* is $f_c - f_s$ *i.e.* the difference between carrier and signal frequencies.

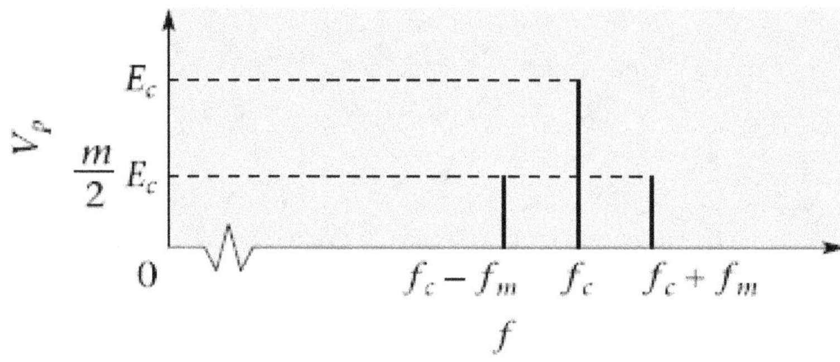

Fig: Side band frequencies with carrier

$$f_{usb} = f_c + f_m$$
$$f_{lsb} = f_c - f_m$$
$$E_{lsb} = E_{usb} = \frac{mE_c}{2}$$

BANDWIDTH OF FCAM SIGNAL

Signal bandwidth is an important characteristic of any modulation scheme. In general, a narrow bandwidth is desirable. Bandwidth of FCAM is calculated by:

$$B = 2F_m$$

Problem-3.5:

a) *A 1-MHz carrier with an amplitude of 1 volt peak is modulated by a 1-kHz signal with m=0.5. Sketch the voltage spectrum.*
b) *An additional 2-kHz signal modulates the carrier with m=0.2. Sketch the voltage spectrum.*

(a) The frequency scale is easy. There are three frequency components. The carrier is at:

$$f_c = 1 \text{ MHz}$$

The upper sideband is at:

$$\begin{aligned} f_{usb} &= f_c + f_m \\ &= 1 \text{ MHz} + 1 \text{ kHz} \\ &= 1.001 \text{ MHz} \end{aligned}$$

The lower sideband is at:

$$\begin{aligned} f_{lsb} &= f_c - f_m \\ &= 1 \text{ MHz} - 1 \text{ kHz} \\ &= 0.999 \text{ MHz} \end{aligned}$$

Next we have to determine the amplitudes of the three components. The car-rier is unchanged with modulation, so it remains at 1 V peak. The two sidebands have the same peak voltage:

$$\begin{aligned} E_{lsb} = E_{usb} &= \frac{mE_c}{2} \\ &= \frac{0.5 \times 1}{2} \\ &= 0.25 \ V \end{aligned}$$

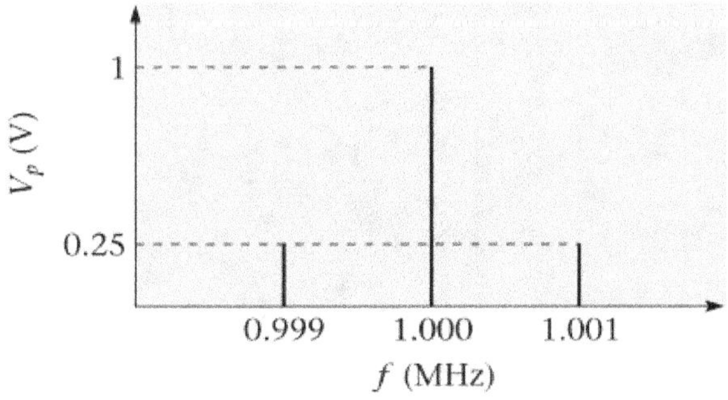

(a) $f_c = 1 \text{ MHz} \quad f_m = 1 \text{ kHz} \quad m = 0.5 \quad E_c = 1 \text{ V}$

(b) The addition of another modulating signal at a different frequency simply adds another set of side frequencies. It does not change anything that was done in part (a). The new frequency components are at 1.002 and 0.998 MHz, and their amplitude is 0.1 volt. The result is shown in Figure b.

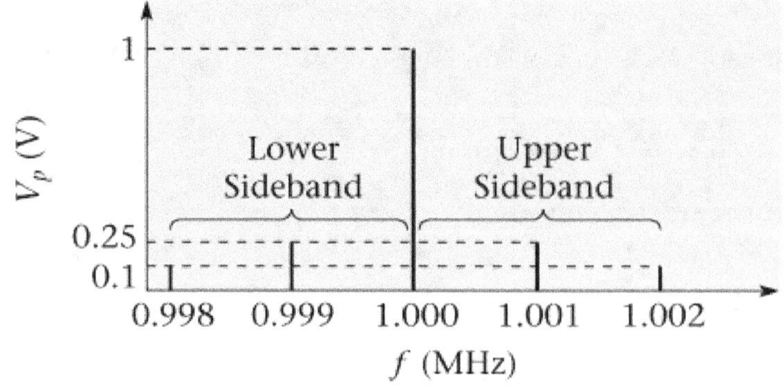

(b) $f_c = 1$ MHz $E_c = 1$ V $f_{m_1} = 1$ kHz $m_1 = 0.5$
$f_{m_2} = 2$ kHz $m_2 = 0.2$

Problem-3.6: Citizens' band radio channels are 10 kHz wide. What is the maximum modulation frequency that can be used if a signal is to remain entirely within its assigned channel?

$$B = 2 F_m$$

so

$$F_m = \frac{B}{2}$$

$$= \frac{10 \text{ kHz}}{2}$$

$$= 5 \text{ kHz}$$

3.1.4 POWER RELATIONSHIPS

The power in the carrier is easy to calculate, since the carrier by itself is a sine wave. The carrier is given by the equation

$$e_c = E_c \sin \omega_c t$$

where

e_c = instantaneous carrier voltage
E_c = peak carrier voltage
ω_c = carrier frequency in radians per second

Since Ec is the peak carrier voltage, the power developed when this signal appears across a resistance R is simply

$$P_c = \frac{\left(\dfrac{E_c}{\sqrt{2}}\right)^2}{R}$$

$$= \frac{E_c^2}{2R}$$

The next step is to find the power in each sideband. The two frequency components have the same amplitude, so they have equal power. Assuming sine-wave modulation, each sideband is a cosine wave whose peak voltage is given by Equation

$$E_{lsb} = E_{usb} = mE_c/2$$

Since the carrier and both sidebands are part of the same signal, the sidebands appear across the same resistance, R, as the carrier. Looking at the lower sideband,

$$P_{lsb} = \frac{E_{lsb}^2}{2R}$$

$$= \frac{\left(\dfrac{mE_c}{2}\right)^2}{2R}$$

$$= \frac{m^2 E_c^2}{4 \times 2R}$$

$$= \frac{m^2}{4} \times \frac{E_c^2}{2R}$$

$$P_{lsb} = P_{usb} = \frac{m^2}{4} P_c$$

Since the two sidebands have equal power, the total sideband power is given by

$$P_{sb} = \frac{m^2}{2} P_c$$

The total power in the whole signal is just the sum of the power in the carrier and the sidebands, so it is

$$P_t = P_c + \left(\frac{m^2}{2}\right)P_c$$

or

$$P_t = P_c\left(1 + \frac{m^2}{2}\right)$$

These latest equations tell us several useful things:

- ➤ The total power in an AM signal increases with modulation, reaching a value 50% greater than that of the unmodulated carrier for 100% modulation.
- ➤ The extra power with modulation goes into the sidebands: the carrier power does not change with modulation.
- ➤ The useful power, that is, the power that carries information, is rather small, being a maximum of one-third of the total signal power for 100% modulation and much less at lower modulation indices. For this reason, AM transmission is more efficient when the modulation index is as close to 1 as practicable.

Problem-3.7: An AM transmitter has a carrier power output of 50 W. What would be the total power produced with 80% modulation?

SOLUTION

$$P_t = P_c\left(1 + \frac{m^2}{2}\right)$$

$$= 50 \text{ W}\left(1 + \frac{0.8^2}{2}\right)$$

$$= 66 \text{ W}$$

3.2 AM Modulators

In this chapter, let us discuss about the modulators, which generate amplitude modulated wave. The following two modulators generate AM wave.

1. Square law modulator
2. Switching modulator

3.2.1 Square Law Modulator

The block diagram of the square law modulator is shown in figure.

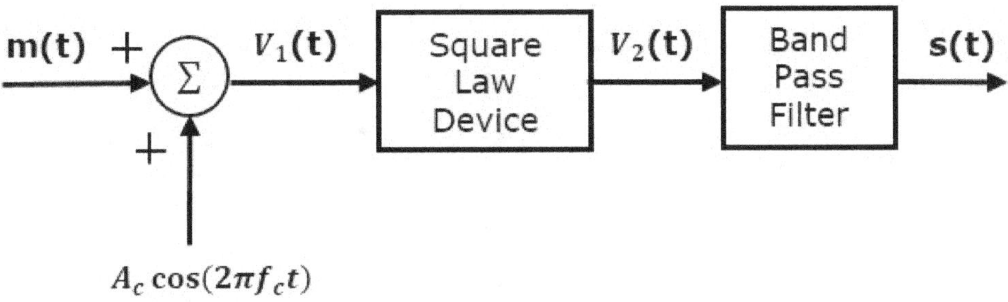

Fig: Square law modulator

Let the modulating and carrier signals be denoted as $m(t)$ and $A\cos(2\pi fct)$ respectively. These two signals are applied as inputs to the summer (adder) block. This summer block produces an output, which is the addition of the modulating and the carrier signal. Mathematically, we can write it as

$$V_1 t = m(t) + A_c \cos(2\pi f_c t)$$

This signal $V_1 t$ is applied as an input to a nonlinear device like diode. The characteristics of the diode are closely related to square law.

$$V_2 t = k_1 V_1(t) + k_2 V_1^2(t) \qquad \text{(Equation 1)}$$

Where, k_1 and k_2 are constants.

Substitute $V_1(t)$ in Equation 1

$$V_2(t) = k_1 \left[m(t) + A_c \cos(2\pi f_c t) \right] + k_2 \left[m(t) + A_c \cos(2\pi f_c t) \right]^2$$

$$\Rightarrow V_2(t) = k_1 m(t) + k_1 A_c \cos(2\pi f_c t) + k_2 m^2(t) +$$
$$k_2 A_c^2 \cos^2(2\pi f_c t) + 2k_2 m(t) A_c \cos(2\pi f_c t)$$

$$\Rightarrow V_2(t) = k_1 m(t) + k_2 m^2(t) + k_2 A_c^2 \cos^2(2\pi f_c t) +$$
$$k_1 A_c \left[1 + \left(\tfrac{2k_2}{k_1} \right) m(t) \right] \cos(2\pi f_c t)$$

The last term of the above equation represents the desired AM wave and the first three terms of the above equation are unwanted. So, with the help of band pass filter, we can pass only AM wave and eliminate the first three terms.

Therefore, the output of square law modulator is

$$s\left(t\right)=k_{1}A_{c}\left[1+\left(\frac{2k_{2}}{k_{1}}\right)m\left(t\right)\right]\cos(2\pi f_{c}t)$$

The standard equation of AM wave is

$$s\left(t\right)=A_{c}\left[1+k_{a}m\left(t\right)\right]\cos(2\pi f_{c}t)$$

Where, K_{a} is the amplitude sensitivity

By comparing the output of the square law modulator with the standard equation of AM wave, we will get the scaling factor as $k1$ and the amplitude sensitivity ka as $\dfrac{2k2}{k1}$

3.2.2 SWITCHING MODULATOR

Following is the block diagram of switching modulator.

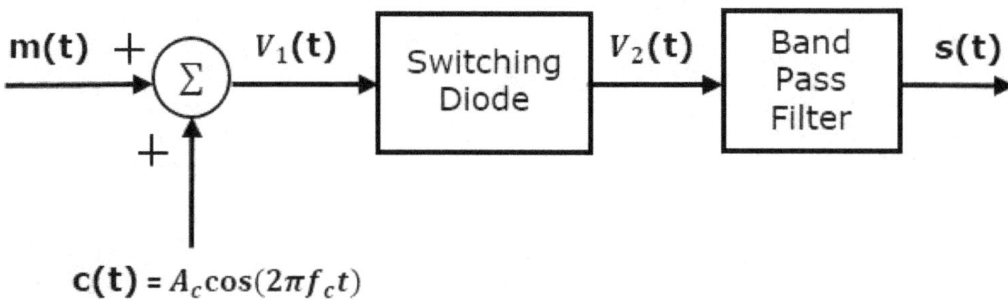

Fig: Switching Modulator

Switching modulator is similar to the square law modulator. The only difference is that in the square law modulator, the diode is operated in a non-linear mode, whereas, in the switching modulator, the diode has to operate as an ideal switch.

Let the modulating and carrier signals be denoted as $m(t)$ and $c(t)=Ac\cos(2\pi fct)$ respectively. These two signals are applied as inputs to the summer (adder) block. Summer block produces an output, which is the addition of modulating and carrier signals. Mathematically, we can write it as

$$V_1\left(t\right) = m\left(t\right) + c\left(t\right) = m\left(t\right) + A_c\cos(2\pi f_c t)$$

This signal $V_1(t)$ is applied as an input of diode. Assume, the magnitude of the modulating signal is very small when compared to the amplitude of carrier signal A_c. So, the diode's ON and OFF action is controlled by carrier signal $c(t)$. This means, the diode will be forward biased when $c(t)>0$ and it will be reverse biased when $c(t)<0$.

Therefore, the output of the diode is

$$V_2\left(t\right) = \begin{cases} V_1\left(t\right) & if \quad c\left(t\right) > 0 \\ 0 & if \quad c\left(t\right) < 0 \end{cases}$$

We can approximate this as

$$V_2\left(t\right) = V_1\left(t\right)\,x\left(t\right) \qquad\qquad \text{(Equation 2)}$$

Where, $x(t)$ is a periodic pulse train with time period $T=1/fc$

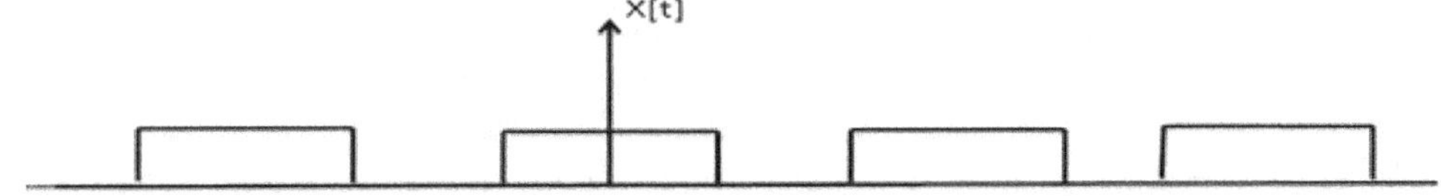

The Fourier series representation of this periodic pulse train is

$$x\left(t\right) = \frac{1}{2} + \frac{2}{\pi}\sum_{n=1}^{\infty}\frac{(-1)^n - 1}{2n - 1}\cos(2\pi\left(2n - 1\right)f_c t)$$

$$\Rightarrow x\left(t\right) = \frac{1}{2} + \frac{2}{\pi}\cos(2\pi f_c t) - \frac{2}{3\pi}\cos(6\pi f_c t) + \ldots$$

Substitute, $V1(t)$ and $x(t)$ values in Equation 2.

$$V_2\left(t\right) = \left[m\left(t\right) + A_c\cos(2\pi f_c t)\right]\left[\tfrac{1}{2} + \tfrac{2}{\pi}\cos(2\pi f_c t) - \tfrac{2}{3\pi}\cos(6\pi f_c t) + \ldots\ldots\right]$$

$$V_2\left(t\right) = \tfrac{m(t)}{2} + \tfrac{A_c}{2}\cos(2\pi f_c t) + \tfrac{2m(t)}{\pi}\cos(2\pi f_c t) + \tfrac{2A_c}{\pi}\cos^2(2\pi f_c t) -$$

$$\tfrac{2m(t)}{3\pi}\cos(6\pi f_c t) - \tfrac{2A_c}{3\pi}\cos(2\pi f_c t)\cos(6\pi f_c t) + \ldots\ldots$$

$$V_2\left(t\right) = \tfrac{A_c}{2}\left(1 + \left(\tfrac{4}{\pi A_c}\right)m\left(t\right)\right)\cos(2\pi f_c t) + \tfrac{m(t)}{2} + \tfrac{2A_c}{\pi}\cos^2(2\pi f_c t) -$$

$$\tfrac{2m(t)}{3\pi}\cos(6\pi f_c t) - \tfrac{2A_c}{3\pi}\cos(2\pi f_c t)\cos(6\pi f_c t) + \ldots\ldots$$

The 1st term of the above equation represents the desired AM wave and the remaining terms are unwanted terms. Thus, with the help of band pass filter, we can pass only AM wave and eliminate the remaining terms.

Therefore, the output of switching modulator is

$$s\left(t\right) = \frac{A_c}{2}\left(1 + \left(\frac{4}{\pi A_c}\right)m\left(t\right)\right)\cos(2\pi f_c t)$$

Where, k_a is the amplitude sensitivity.

By comparing the output of the switching modulator with the standard equation of AM wave, we will get the scaling factor as 0.5 and amplitude sensitivity k_a as $\dfrac{4}{\pi A_c}$

3.3 AM Demodulators

The process of extracting an original message signal from the modulated wave is known as detection or demodulation. The circuit, which demodulates the modulated wave is known as the demodulator. The following demodulators (detectors) are used for demodulating AM wave.

1) Square Law Demodulator
2) Envelope Detector

3.3.1 Square Law Demodulator

Square law demodulator is used to demodulate low level AM wave. Following is the block diagram of the square law demodulator.

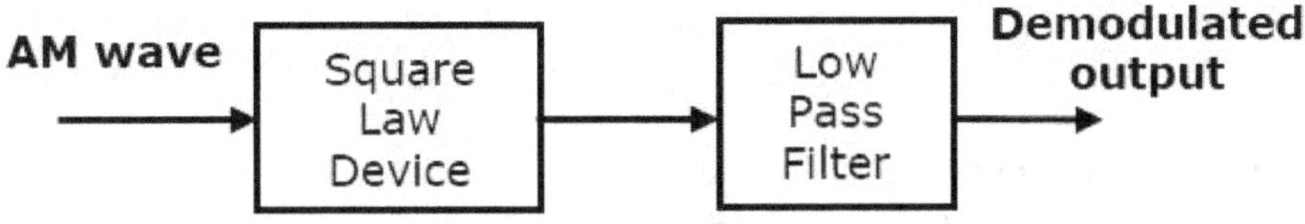

Fig: Square law demodulator

This demodulator contains a square law device and low pass filter. The AM wave $V_1(t)$ is applied as an input to this demodulator.

The standard form of AM wave is

$$V_1(t) = A_c\left[1 + k_a m(t)\right]\cos(2\pi f_c t)$$

We know that the mathematical relationship between the input and the output of square law device is

$$V_2(t) = k_1 V_1(t) + k_2 V_1^2(t) \qquad \text{(Equation 1)}$$

Where, $V_1(t)$ is the input of the square law device, which is nothing but the AM wave, $V_2(t)$ is the output of the square law device, k_1 and k_2 are constants

Substitute $V_1(t)$ in Equation 1

$$V_2(t) = k_1\left(A_c\left[1 + k_a m(t)\right]\cos(2\pi f_c t)\right)$$
$$+ k_2\left(A_c\left[1 + k_a m(t)\right]\cos(2\pi f_c t)\right)^2$$

$$\Rightarrow V_2(t) = k_1 A_c \cos(2\pi f_c t) + k_1 A_c k_a m(t)\cos(2\pi f_c t) +$$
$$k_2 A_c^2\left[1 + K_a^2 m^2(t) + 2k_a m(t)\right]\left(\frac{1+\cos(4\pi f_c t)}{2}\right)$$

$$\Rightarrow V_2(t) = k_1 A_c \cos(2\pi f_c t) + k_1 A_c k_a m(t)\cos(2\pi f_c t) + \frac{K_2 A_c^2}{2} +$$
$$\frac{K_2 A_c^2}{2}\cos(4\pi f_c t) + \frac{k_2 A_c^2 k_a^2 m^2(t)}{2} + \frac{k_2 A_c^2 k_a^2 m^2(t)}{2}\cos(4\pi f_c t) +$$
$$k_2 A_c^2 k_a m(t) + k_2 A_c^2 k_a m(t)\cos(4\pi f_c t)$$

In the above equation, the term

$$k_2 A_c^{\;2} k_a m\,(t)$$

is the scaled version of the message signal. It can be extracted by passing the above signal through a low pass filter and the DC component

$$\frac{k_2 A_c^{\;2}}{2}$$

can be eliminated with the help of a coupling capacitor.

3.3.2 ENVELOPE DETECTOR

Envelope detector is used to detect (demodulate) high level AM wave. The block diagram of the envelope detector is shown in figure.

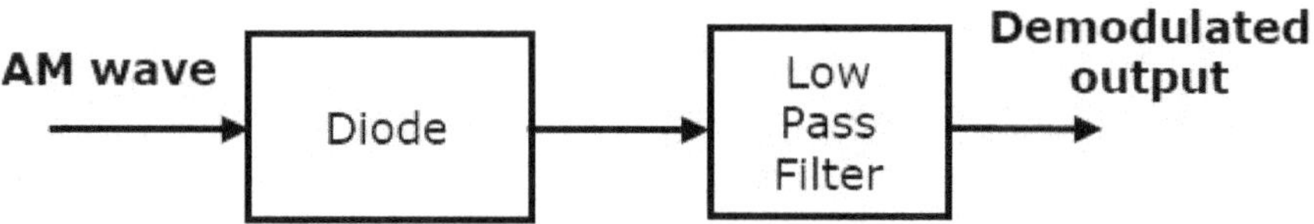

Fig: Envelope Detector

This envelope detector consists of a diode and low pass filter. Here, the diode is the main detecting element. Hence, the envelope detector is also called as the diode detector. The low pass filter contains a parallel combination of the resistor and the capacitor.

The AM wave $s(t)$ is applied as an input to this detector.

We know the standard form of AM wave is

$$s\,(t) = A_c\,[1 + k_a m\,(t)]\cos(2\pi f_c t)$$

In the positive half cycle of AM wave, the diode conducts and the capacitor charges to the peak value of AM wave. When the value of AM wave is less than this value, the diode will be reverse biased. Thus, the capacitor will discharge through resistor R till the next positive half cycle of AM wave. When the value of AM wave is greater than the capacitor voltage, the diode conducts and the process will be repeated.

We should select the component values in such a way that the capacitor charges very quickly and discharges very slowly. As a result, we will get the capacitor voltage waveform same as that of the envelope of AM wave, which is almost similar to the modulating signal.

In the process of Amplitude Modulation, the modulated wave consists of the carrier wave and two sidebands. The modulated wave has the information only in the sidebands. Sideband is nothing but a band of frequencies, containing power, which are the lower and higher frequencies of the carrier frequency.

The transmission of a signal, which contains a carrier along with two sidebands can be termed as Double Sideband Full Carrier system or simply DSBFC. It is plotted as shown in the following figure.

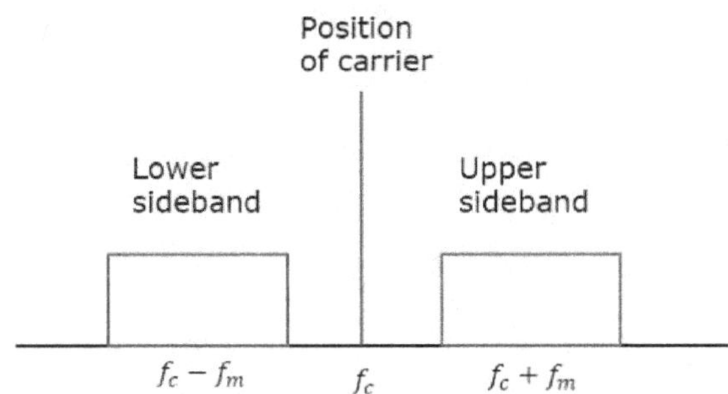

Fig: Double side band full carrier

It is possible to improve the efficiency and reduce the bandwidth of an AM signal by removing the carrier and/or one of its sidebands. The carrier has at least two-thirds of the power in an AM signal, but none of the information. This can be understood by noting that the presence of modulation has no effect on the carrier.

However, such a transmission is inefficient. Because, the two-thirds of the power is being wasted in the carrier, which carries no information.

If this carrier is suppressed and the saved power is distributed to the two sidebands, then such a process is called as Double Sideband Suppressed Carrier system or simply DSBSC. It is plotted as shown in the following figure.

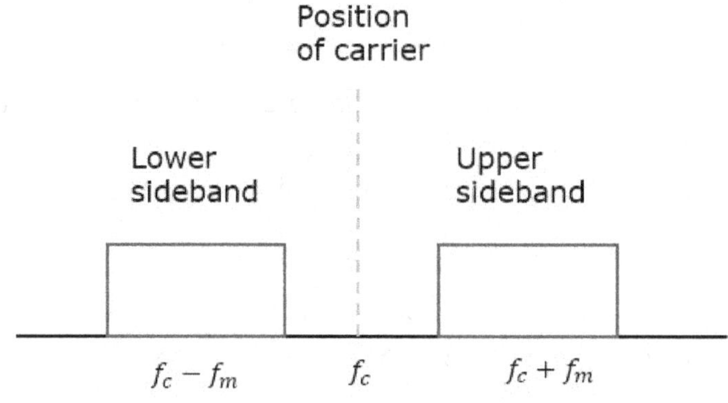

Fig: Double side band suppressed carrier

Mathematical representation:

Let us consider the same mathematical expressions for modulating and carrier signals

Modulating signal

$$m(t)=A_m\cos(2\pi f_m t)$$

Carrier signal

$$c(t)=A_c\cos(2\pi f_c t)$$

Mathematically, we can represent the equation of DSBSC wave as the product of modulating and carrier signals.

$$s(t)=m(t)c(t)$$

$$\Rightarrow s(t)=A_m A_c\cos(2\pi f_m t)\cos(2\pi f_c t)$$

Bandwidth:

We know the formula for bandwidth (BW) is

$$BW=f_{max}-f_{min}$$

Consider the equation of DSBSC modulated wave.

$$s(t) = A_m A_c \cos(2\pi f_m t)\cos(2\pi f_c t)$$

$$\Rightarrow s(t) = \frac{A_m A_c}{2}\cos[2\pi(f_c + f_m)t] + \frac{A_m A_c}{2}\cos[2\pi(f_c - f_m)t]$$

The DSBSC modulated wave has only two frequencies. So, the maximum and minimum frequencies are $fc+fm$ and $fc-fm$ respectively. i.e., $fmax=fc+fm$ and $fmin=fc-fm$

Substitute, $fmax$ and $fmin$ values in the bandwidth formula.

$$BW=fc+fm-(fc-fm)$$
$$\Rightarrow BW=2fm$$

Thus, the bandwidth of DSBSC wave is same as that of AM wave and it is equal to twice the frequency of the modulating signal.

Power Calculation:

Consider the following equation of DSBSC modulated wave.

$$s(t) = \frac{A_m A_c}{2}\cos[2\pi(f_c + f_m)t] + \frac{A_m A_c}{2}\cos[2\pi(f_c - f_m)t]$$

Power of DSBSC wave is equal to the sum of powers of upper sideband and lower sideband frequency components.

$$Pt=P_{USB}+P_{LSB}$$

We know the standard formula for power of cos signal is

$$P = \frac{v_{rms}^2}{R} = \frac{\left(v_m \sqrt{2}\right)^2}{R}$$

First, let us find the powers of upper sideband and lower sideband one by one.

Upper sideband power

$$P_{USB} = \frac{\left(A_m A_c / 2\sqrt{2}\right)^2}{R} = \frac{A_m{}^2 A_c{}^2}{8R}$$

Similarly, we will get the lower sideband power same as that of upper sideband power.

$$P_{USB} = \frac{A_m{}^2 A_c{}^2}{8R}$$

Now, let us add these two sideband powers in order to get the power of DSBSC wave.

$$P_t = \frac{A_m{}^2 A_c{}^2}{8R} + \frac{A_m{}^2 A_c{}^2}{8R}$$

$$\Rightarrow P_t = \frac{A_m{}^2 A_c{}^2}{4R}$$

Therefore, the power required for transmitting DSBSC wave is equal to the power of both the sidebands.

3.5 SSBSC Modulation

The DSBSC modulated signal has two sidebands. Since, the two sidebands carry the same information, there is no need to transmit both sidebands. We can eliminate one sideband.

The upper and lower sidebands are mirror images of each other, containing exactly the same information. Removing one of these sidebands would reduce the signal bandwidth by half. Assuming that the receiver bandwidth is also reduced by half, this should result in a reduction of the noise power by a factor of two (3 dB). Therefore, removing the carrier and one sideband should cause the resulting single-sideband suppressed-carrier AM (SSBSC or just SSB) signal. It is plotted as shown in the following figure.

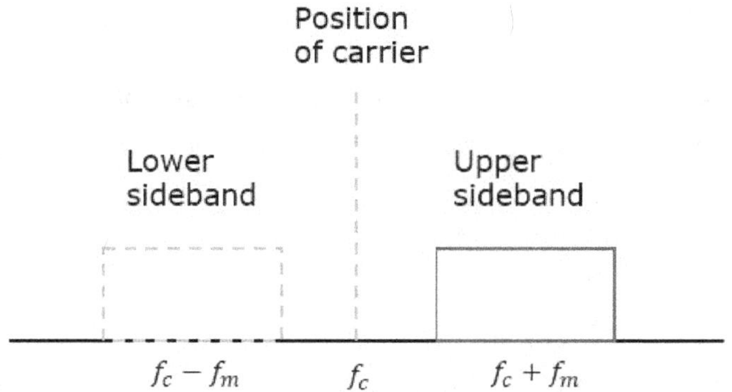

Fig: Single side band suppressed carrier

In the above figure, the carrier and the lower sideband are suppressed. Hence, the upper sideband is used for transmission. Similarly, we can suppress the carrier and the upper sideband while transmitting the lower sideband.

This SSBSC system, which transmits a single sideband has high power, as the power allotted for both the carrier and the other sideband is utilized in transmitting this Single Sideband.

Mathematical Expressions

Let us consider the same mathematical expressions for the modulating and the carrier signals

Modulating signal

$$m(t) = A_m \cos(2\pi f_m t)$$

Carrier signal

$$c(t) = A_c \cos(2\pi f_c t)$$

Mathematically, we can represent the equation of SSBSC wave as

$$s(t) = \frac{A_m A_c}{2} \cos[2\pi (f_c + f_m) t] \qquad \text{for the upper sideband}$$

Or

$$s(t) = \frac{A_m A_c}{2} \cos[2\pi (f_c - f_m) t] \qquad \text{for the lower sideband}$$

Bandwidth of SSBSC Wave

We know that the DSBSC modulated wave contains two sidebands and its bandwidth is $2f_m$. Since the SSBSC modulated wave contains only one sideband, its bandwidth is half of the bandwidth of DSBSC modulated wave.

i.e., Bandwidth of SSBSC modulated wave $= 2f_m/2 = f_m$

Therefore, the bandwidth of SSBSC modulated wave is f_m and it is equal to the frequency of the modulating signal.

Power Calculations of SSBSC Wave

Consider the following equation of SSBSC modulated wave.

$$s(t) = \frac{A_m A_c}{2} \cos[2\pi(f_c + f_m)t] \qquad \text{for the upper sideband}$$

Or

$$s(t) = \frac{A_m A_c}{2} \cos[2\pi(f_c - f_m)t] \qquad \text{for the lower sideband}$$

Power of SSBSC wave is equal to the power of any one sideband frequency components.

$$P_t = P_{USB} = P_{LSB}$$

We know that the standard formula for power of cos signal is

$$P = \frac{v_{rms}^2}{R} = \frac{\left(v_m/\sqrt{2}\right)^2}{R}$$

In this case, the power of the upper sideband is

$$P_{USB} = \frac{\left(A_m A_c/2\sqrt{2}\right)^2}{R} = \frac{A_m^2 A_c^2}{8R}$$

Similarly, we will get the lower sideband power same as that of the upper side band power.

$$P_{LSB} = \frac{A_m^2 A_c^2}{8R}$$

Therefore, the power of SSBSC wave is

$$P_t = P_{USB} = P_{LSB} = \frac{A_m{}^2 A_c{}^2}{8R}$$

Advantages

- Bandwidth or spectrum space occupied is lesser than AM and DSBSC waves.
- Transmission of more number of signals is allowed.
- Power is saved.
- High power signal can be transmitted.
- Less amount of noise is present.
- Signal fading is less likely to occur.

Disadvantages

- The generation and detection of SSBSC wave is a complex process.
- The quality of the signal gets affected unless the SSB transmitter and receiver have an excellent frequency stability.

Applications

- For power saving requirements and low bandwidth requirements.
- In land, air, and maritime mobile communications.
- In point-to-point communications.
- In radio communications.
- In television, telemetry, and radar communications.
- In military communications, such as amateur radio, etc.

3.6 VSBSC Modulation

In the previous sections, we have discussed SSBSC modulation and demodulation. SSBSC modulated signal has only one sideband frequency. Theoretically, we can get one sideband frequency component completely by using an ideal band pass filter. However, practically we may not get the entire sideband frequency component. Due to this, some information gets lost.

To avoid this loss, a technique is chosen, which is a compromise between DSBSC and SSBSC. This technique is known as Vestigial Side Band Suppressed Carrier (VSBSC) technique. The word "vestige" means "a part" from which, the name is derived.

VSBSC Modulation is the process, where a part of the signal called as vestige is modulated along with one sideband. The frequency spectrum of VSBSC wave is shown in the following figure 15.

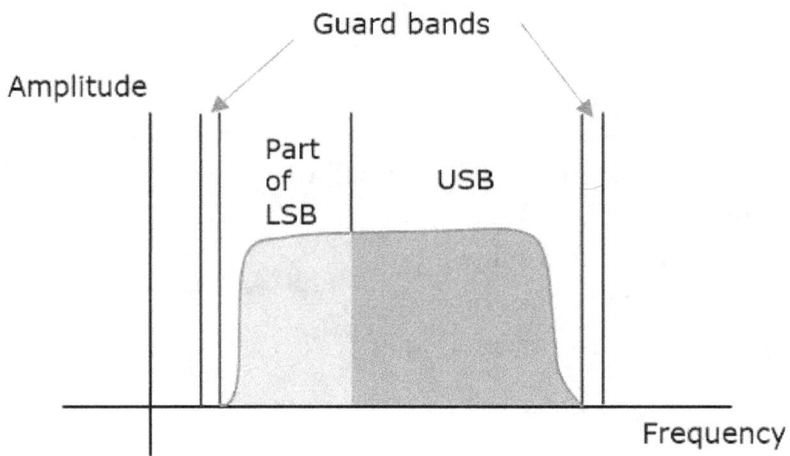

Along with the upper sideband, a part of the lower sideband is also being transmitted in this technique. Similarly, we can transmit the lower sideband along with a part of the upper sideband. A guard band of very small width is laid on either side of VSB in order to avoid the interferences. VSB modulation is mostly used in television transmissions.

Bandwidth of VSBSC Modulation

We know that the bandwidth of SSBSC modulated wave is f_m. Since the VSBSC modulated wave contains the frequency components of one side band along with the vestige of other sideband, the bandwidth of it will be the sum of the bandwidth of SSBSC modulated wave and vestige frequency f_v.

i.e., Bandwidth of VSBSC Modulated Wave $= f_m + f_v$

Advantages:

Following are the advantages of VSBSC modulation.

- Highly efficient.
- Reduction in bandwidth when compared to AM and DSBSC waves.
- Filter design is easy, since high accuracy is not needed.
- The transmission of low frequency components is possible, without any difficulty.
- Possesses good phase characteristics.

Disadvantages

Following are the disadvantages of VSBSC modulation.

- Bandwidth is more when compared to SSBSC wave.
- Demodulation is complex.

Applications

The most prominent and standard application of VSBSC is for the transmission of television signals. Also, this is the most convenient and efficient technique when bandwidth usage is considered.

Now, let us discuss about the modulator which generates VSBSC wave and the demodulator which demodulates VSBSC wave one by one.

Problem-3.8: A signal Am Sin fm π t and carrier is Ac sin($2\pi fc$ t + ∂). Find the DSB, Amplitude modulated signal and draw the upper and lower sideband frequency spectrum.

Message signal = A_m Sin $f_m \pi$ t

Carrier Signal = A_c sin($2\pi f_c$ t + ∂).

DSB, Amplitude modulated signal = [A_m Sin $f_m \pi$ t] * [A_c Sin($2\pi f_c$ t + ∂)]

$$= A_m A_c * \text{Sin } f_m \pi t * \text{Sin}(2\pi f_c t + \partial)$$
$$= (A_m A_c/2)*[2 \text{ Sin } f_m \pi t * \text{ Sin}(2\pi f_c t + \partial)]$$
$$= (A_m A_c/2)*[2 \text{ Sin}(2\pi f_c t + \partial)* \text{ Sin } f_m \pi t]$$
$$- (A_m A_c/2)*[\text{Cos } (2\pi f_c t + \partial - f_m \pi t) - \text{Cos } (2\pi f_c t + \partial + f_m \pi t)$$
$$= (A_m A_c/2)*[\text{Cos } \{(2\pi f_c t + \partial - f_m \pi t) - \text{Cos } (2\pi f_c t + \partial + f_m \pi t)$$

Problem-3.9:

Draw the frequency spectrum of x(t) and y(t):

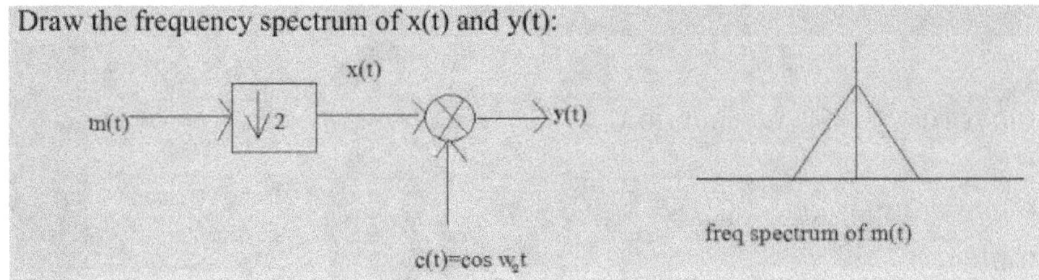

Solution:

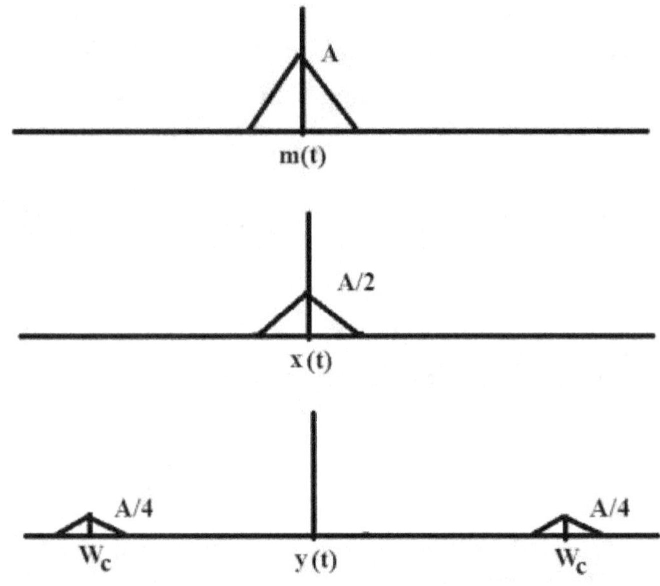

Problem-3.10:

The spectrum of a modulating signal is shown in the figure. Draw the spectrum of DSB-SC, SSB+C, and VSB modulated signals for this modulating signal assuming a carrier signal of $C(t) = A_C \cos 2\pi f_C' t$

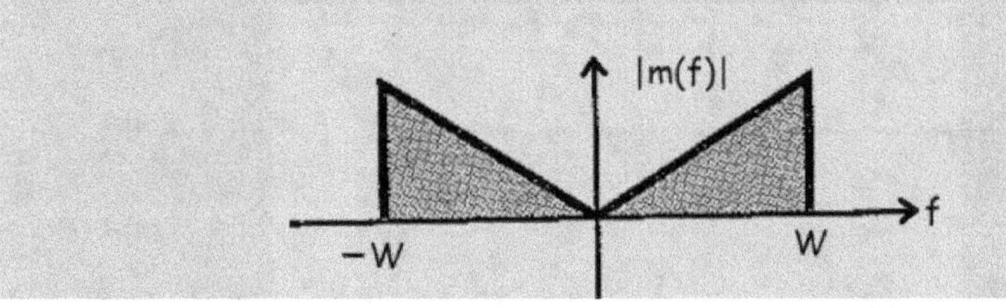

Solution:

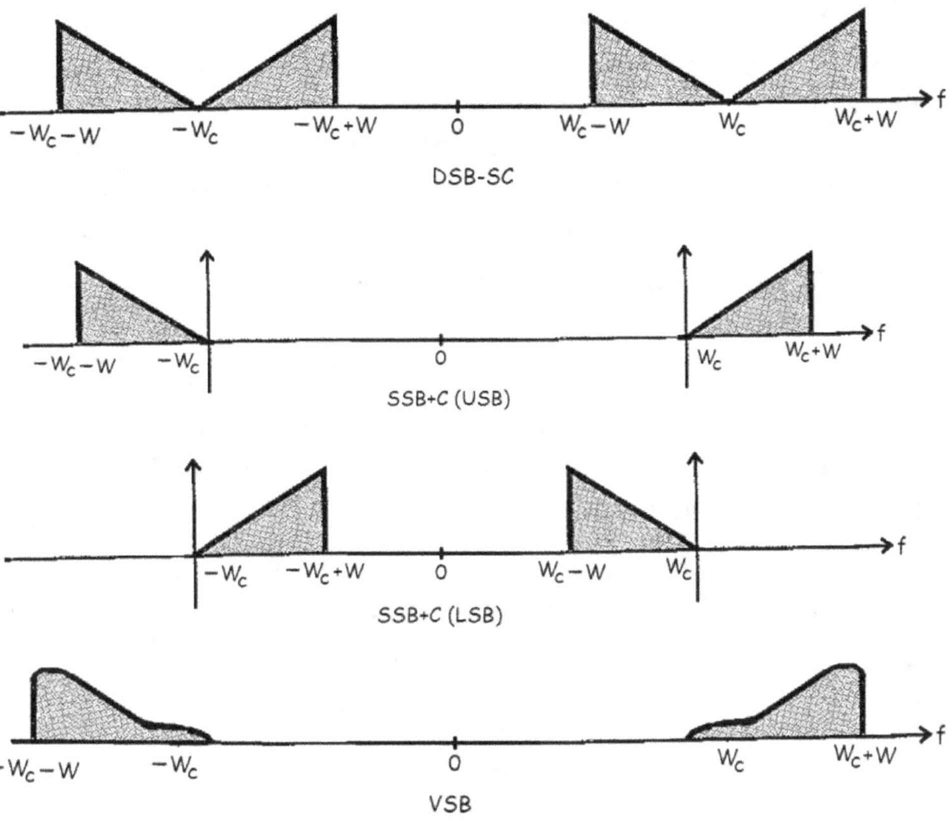

Problem-3.11:

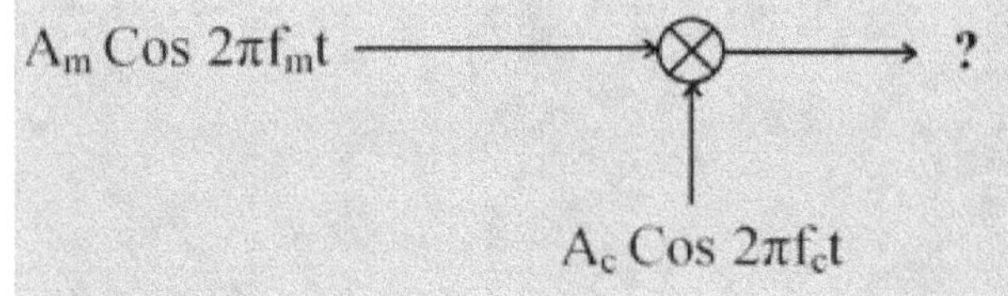

<u>*Solution:*</u>

$$\begin{aligned}
\text{Output} &= A_m \cos 2\pi f_m t * A_c \cos 2\pi f_c t \\
&= (A_m A_c/2)*[2\ \cos 2\pi f_m t * \cos 2\pi f_c t] \\
&= (A_m A_c/2)*[\cos(2\pi f_c t + 2\pi f_m t) + \cos(2\pi f_c t - 2\pi f_m t)] \\
&= (A_m A_c/2)*[\cos 2\pi (f_c + f_m)t + \cos 2\pi (f_c - f_m)t]\ \underline{\textbf{Ans.}}
\end{aligned}$$

Problem-3.12: A 2500 kHz carrier is modulated by audio signal with frequency span of 50 −15000 Hz. What are the frequencies of lower and upper sidebands? What bandwidth of RF amplifier is required to handle the output?

Solution. The modulating signal (*e.g.* music) has a range of 0.05 to 15 kHz. The sideband frequencies produced range from $f_c \pm 0.05$ kHz to $f_c \pm 15$ kHz. Therefore, upper sideband ranges from 2500.05 to 2515 kHz and lower sideband ranges from 2499.95 to 2485 kHz.

The sideband frequencies produced can be approximately expressed as 2500 ± 15 kHz. Therefore, bandwidth requirement $= 2515 - 2485 = 30$ kHz. Note that bandwidth of *RF* amplifier required is twice the frequency of highest modulating signal frequency.

Problem-3.13: An AM wave is represented by the expression:

$$v = 5\,(1 + 0.6\cos 6280\,t)\sin 211 \times 10^4\,t\ volts$$

i.   ***What are the minimum and maximum amplitudes of the AM wave?***

ii.   ***What frequency components are contained in the modulated wave and what is the amplitude of each component?***

Solution.

The AM wave equation is given by : $v = 5\,(1 + 0.6\cos 6280\,t)\sin 211 \times 10^4\,t\ volts$ ...(*i*)

Compare it with standard AM wave eq., $v = E_C\,(1 + m\cos \omega_s\,t)\sin \omega_c\,t$ ...(*ii*)

From eqs. (*i*) and (*ii*) , we get,

$$E_C = \text{carrier amplitude} = 5\ V$$
$$m = \text{modulation factor} = 0.6$$
$$f_s = \text{signal frequency} = \omega_s/2\pi = 6280/2\pi = 1\ \text{kHz}$$
$$f_c = \text{carrier frequency} = \omega_c/2\pi = 211 \times 10^4/2\pi = 336\ \text{kHz}$$

(*i*) Minimum amplitude of AM wave $= E_C - mE_C = 5 - 0.6 \times 5 = 2\ V$

      Maximum amplitude of AM wave $= E_C + mE_C = 5 + 0.6 \times 5 = 8\ V$

(*ii*) The AM wave will contain three frequencies *viz.*

	$f_c - f_s$,	f_c,	$f_c + f_s$
or	$336 - 1$,	336,	$336 + 1$
or	335 kHz,	336 kHz,	337 kHz

The amplitudes of the three components of AM wave are :

	$\dfrac{mE_C}{2}$,	E_C,	$\dfrac{mE_C}{2}$
or	$\dfrac{0.6 \times 5}{2}$,	5,	$\dfrac{0.6 \times 5}{2}$
or	1.5 V,	5 V,	1.5 V

Problem-3.14: *A sinusoidal carrier voltage of frequency 1 MHz and amplitude 100 volts is amplitude modulated by sinusoidal voltage of frequency 5 kHz producing 50% modulation. Calculate the frequency and amplitude of lower and upper sideband terms.*

Solution.

$$\text{Frequency of carrier, } f_c = 1 \text{ MHz} = 1000 \text{ kHz}$$
$$\text{Frequency of signal, } f_s = 5 \text{ kHz}$$
$$\text{Modulation factor, } m = 50\% = 0.5$$

$$\text{Amplitude of carrier, } E_C = 100 \text{ V}$$

The lower and upper sideband frequencies are :

$$f_c - f_s \quad \text{and} \quad f_c + f_s$$

or $(1000 - 5)$ kHz and $(1000 + 5)$ kHz

or 995 kHz and 1005 kHz

$$\text{Amplitude of each sideband term} = \frac{mE_C}{2} = \frac{0.5 \times 100}{2} = 25 \text{ V}$$

Problem-3.15: *A carrier wave of frequency 10 MHz and peak value 10V is amplitude modulated by a 5- kHz sine wave of amplitude 6V. Determine*

i. *modulation factor*
ii. *sideband frequencies and*
iii. *amplitude of sideband components.*

Draw the frequency spectrum.

Solution.

$$\text{Carrier amplitude, } E_C = 10\text{V}$$
$$\text{Signal amplitude, } E_S = 6\text{V}$$
$$\text{Carrier frequency, } f_c = 10 \text{ MHz}$$
$$\text{Signal frequency, } f_s = 5 \text{ kHz} = 0.005 \text{ MHz}$$

(i) Modulation factor, $m = \dfrac{E_S}{E_C} = \dfrac{6}{10} = 0.6$

(ii) Sideband frequencies are :

$$f_c - f_s \;\; ; \;\; f_c + f_s$$
$$10 - 0.005 \;\; ; \;\; 10 + 0.005$$
$$9.995 \text{ MHz} \;\; ; \;\; 10.005 \text{ MHz}$$

(iii) Amplitude of each sideband $= \dfrac{m\,E_C}{2} = \dfrac{0.6 \times 10}{2} = 3\text{V}$

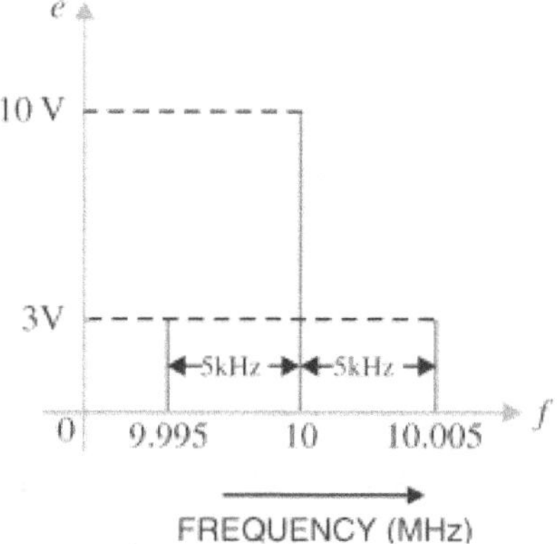

3.7 POWER IN AM WAVE

The power dissipated in any circuit is a function of the square of voltage across the circuit and the effective resistance of the circuit. Equation of AM wave reveals that it has three components of amplitude E_C, $m\,E_C/2$ and $m\,E_C/2$. Clearly, power output must be distributed among these components.

$$\text{Carrier power,} \quad P_C = \frac{\left(E_C/\sqrt{2}\right)^2}{R} = \frac{E_C^2}{2R} \qquad \ldots(i)$$

$$\text{Total power of sidebands,} \quad P_S = \frac{\left(m\,E_C/2\sqrt{2}\right)^2}{R} + \frac{\left(m\,E_C/2\sqrt{2}\right)^2}{R}$$

$$= \frac{m^2\,E_C^2}{8R} + \frac{m^2\,E_C^2}{8R} = \frac{m^2\,E_C^2}{4R} \qquad \ldots(ii)$$

$$\text{Total power of AM wave,} \quad P_T = P_C + P_S$$

$$= \frac{E_C^2}{2R} + \frac{m^2\,E_C^2}{4R} = \frac{E_C^2}{2R}\left[1 + \frac{m^2}{2}\right]$$

$$\text{or} \qquad P_T = \frac{E_C^2}{2R}\,\frac{\left[2 + m^2\right]}{2} \qquad \ldots(iii)$$

Fraction of total power carried by sidebands is

$$\frac{P_S}{P_T} = \frac{\text{Exp. }(ii)}{\text{Exp. }(iii)} = \frac{m^2}{2 + m^2} \qquad \ldots(iv)$$

As the signal is contained in the sideband frequencies, therefore, useful power is in the sidebands. Inspection of exp. (iv) reveals that sideband power depends upon the modulation factor m. The greater the value of m, the greater is the useful power carried by the sidebands. This emphasises the importance of modulation factor.

(i) When $m = 0$, power carried by sidebands $= 0^2/2 + 0^2 = 0$

(ii) When $m = 0.5$, power carried by sidebands

$$= \frac{(0.5)^2}{2 + (0.5)^2} = 11.1\,\% \text{ of total power of AM wave}$$

(iii) When $m = 1$, power carried by sidebands

$$= \frac{(1)^2}{2 + (1)^2} = 33.3\% \text{ of total power of AM wave}$$

As an example, suppose the total power of an AM wave is 600 watts and modulation is 100%. Then sideband power is 600/3 = 200 watts and carrier power will be $600 - 200 = 400$ watts.

The sideband power represents the signal content and the carrier power is that power which is required as the means of transmission.

3.7.1 RELATION BETWEEN TOTAL SIDEBAND POWER AND CARRIER POWER

$$P_C = \frac{E_C^2}{2R} \quad \text{and} \quad P_S = \frac{m^2 E_C^2}{4R}$$

$$\frac{P_S}{P_C} = \frac{1}{2} m^2$$

$$P_S = \frac{1}{2} m^2 P_C$$

3.8 LIMITATIONS OF AMPLITUDE MODULATION

Although theoretically highly effective, amplitude modulation suffers from the following drawbacks:

i. **Noisy reception**: In an AM wave, the signal is in the amplitude variations of the carrier. Practically all the natural and man made noises consist of electrical amplitude disturbances. As a radio receiver cannot distinguish between amplitude variations that represent noise and those that contain the desired signal, therefore, reception is generally noisy.

ii. **Low efficiency:** In amplitude modulation, useful power is in the sidebands as they contain the signal. As discussed before, an AM wave has low sideband power. For example, if modulation is 100%, the sideband power is only one-third of the total power of AM wave. Hence the efficiency of this type of modulation is low.

iii. **Small operating range:** Due to low efficiency of amplitude modulation, transmitters employing this method have a small operating range i.e. messages cannot be transmitted over larger distances.

iv. **Lack of audio quality:** This is a distinct disadvantage of amplitude modulation. In order to attain high-fidelity reception, all audio frequencies up to 15 kHz must be reproduced. This necessitates bandwidth of 30 kHz since both sidebands must be reproduced. But AM broadcasting stations are assigned bandwidth of only 10 kHz to minimise the interference from adjacent broadcasting stations. This means that the highest modulating frequency can be 5 kHz which is hardly sufficient to reproduce the music properly.

Problem-3.16: A carrier wave of 500 watts is subjected to 100% amplitude modulation. Determine

 i. *power in sidebands*
 ii. *power of modulated wave.*

Solution.

(i) Sideband power, $P_S = \dfrac{1}{2} m^2 P_C = \dfrac{1}{2} \times 500 = 250$ W

Thus there are 125 W in upper sideband and 125 W in lower sideband.

(ii) Power of AM wave, $P_T = P_C + P_S = 500 + 250 = 750$ W

Problem-3.17: A 50 kW carrier is to be modulated to a level of (i) 80% (ii)10%. What is the total sideband power in each case?

Solution. (i) $P_S = \dfrac{1}{2} m^2 P_C = \dfrac{1}{2} (0.8)^2 \times 50 = 16$ kW

(ii) $P_S = \dfrac{1}{2} m^2 P_C = \dfrac{1}{2} (0.1)^2 \times 50 = 0.25$ kW

Problem-3.18: A 40kW carrier is to be modulated to a level of 100%.

 i. *What is the carrier power after modulation?*
 ii. *How much audio power is required if the efficiency of the modulated RF amplifier is 72%?*

Solution. Fig. 16.10 shows the block diagram indicating the power relations.

(i) Since the carrier itself is unaffected by the modulating signal, there is no change in the carrier power level.

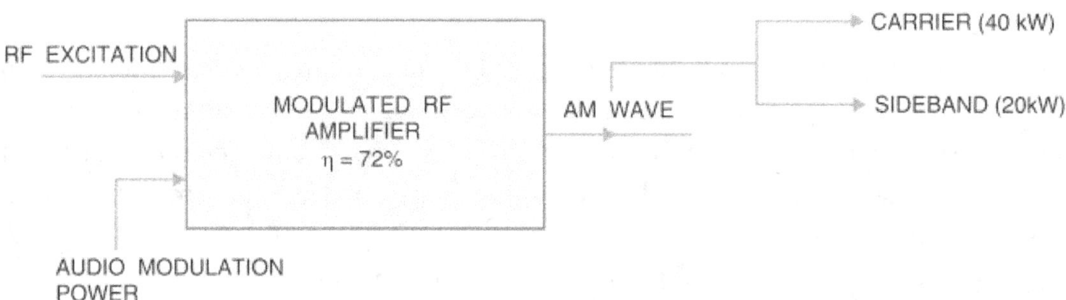

∴ $P_C = 40$ kW

(ii) $P_S = \dfrac{1}{2} m^2 P_C = \dfrac{1}{2} (1)^2 \times 40 = 20$ kW

∴ $P_{audio} = \dfrac{P_S}{0.72} = \dfrac{20}{0.72} = 27.8$ kW

Problem-3.19: *An audio signal of 1 kHz is used to modulate a carrier of 500 kHz. Determine*

   i.   **sideband frequencies**

   ii.   **bandwidth required.**

Solution.   Carrier frequency, f_c = 500 kHz

                 Signal frequency, f_s = 1 kHz

(i) As discussed in Art. 16.6, the *AM* wave has sideband frequencies of $(f_c + f_s)$ and $(f_c - f_s)$.

$\therefore$ Sideband frequencies = (500 + 1) kHz and (500 − 1) kHz

                        = 501 kHz and 499 kHz

(ii)   Bandwidth required = 499 kHz to 501 kHz = 2 kHz

Problem-3.20: *The load current in the transmitting antenna of an unmodulated AM transmitter is 8A. What will be the antenna current when modulation is 40%?*

Solution.

$$P_S = \frac{1}{2} m^2 P_C$$

$$P_T = P_C + P_S = P_C \left(1 + \frac{m^2}{2}\right)$$

$$\therefore \quad \frac{P_T}{P_C} = 1 + \frac{m^2}{2}$$

or

$$\left(\frac{I_T}{I_C}\right)^2 = 1 + \frac{m^2}{2}$$

Given that I_C = 8A; m = 0.4

$$\therefore \quad \left(\frac{I_T}{8}\right)^2 = 1 + \frac{(0.4)^2}{2}$$

or

$$(I_T/8)^2 = 1.08$$

or

$$I_T = 8\sqrt{1.08} = 8.31 \text{ A}$$

Problem-3.21: *The r.m.s. value of carrier voltage is 100 V. After amplitude modulation by a sinusoidal a.f. voltage, the r.m.s. value becomes 110 V. Calculate the modulation index.*

Solution.

$$\frac{P_T}{P_C} = 1 + \frac{m^2}{2}$$

or

$$\left(\frac{V_T}{V_C}\right)^2 = 1 + \frac{m^2}{2}$$

Given that V_T = 110 V ; V_C = 100 V ; m = ?

$$\therefore \quad \left(\frac{110}{100}\right)^2 = 1 + \frac{m^2}{2}$$

or

$$1.21 = 1 + \frac{m^2}{2}$$

or

$$m^2/2 = 0.21$$

or

$$m = \sqrt{0.21 \times 2} = 0.648$$

Problem-3.22: An AM wave consists of the following components:

Carrier component = 5 V peak value

Lower sideband component = 2.5 V peak value

Upper sideband component = 2.5 V peak value

If the AM wave drives a 2 kΩ resistor, find the power delivered to the resistor by

    i.   *carrier*
   ii.   *lower sideband component and*
  iii.   *upper sideband component.*

What is the total power delivered?

Solution:

$$\text{Power} = \frac{(\text{r.m.s. voltage})^2}{R} = \frac{(0.707 \times \text{peak value})^2}{R}$$

(i) Power delivered by the carrier, $P_C = \dfrac{(0.707 \times 5)^2}{2000} = 6.25 \text{ mW}$

(ii) Power delivered by lower sideband component is

$$P_{lower} = \frac{(0.707 \times 2.5)^2}{2000} = 1.562 \text{ mW}$$

(iii) Power delivered by upper sideband component is

$$P_{upper} = \frac{(0.707 \times 2.5)^2}{2000} = 1.562 \text{ mW}$$

Total power delivered by the *AM* wave $= 6.25 + 1.562 + 1.562 = 9.374 \text{ mW}$

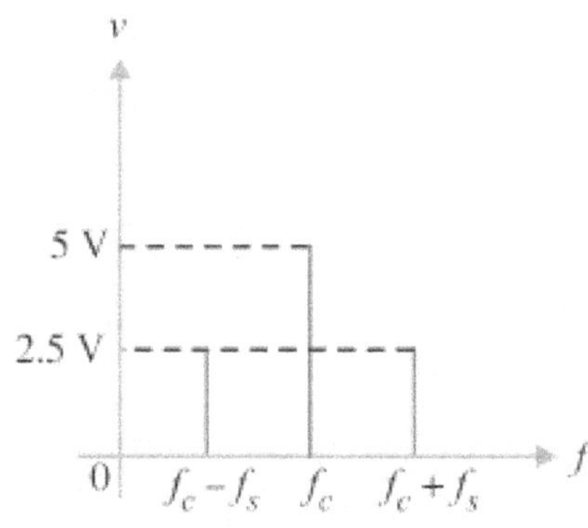

CHAPTER-4

FREQUENCY MODULATION

4.1 FREQUENCY MODULATION (FM)

When the frequency of carrier wave is changed in accordance with the intensity of the signal, it is called frequency modulation (FM).

In frequency modulation, only the frequency of the carrier wave is changed in accordance with the signal. However, the amplitude of the modulated wave remains the same i.e. carrier wave amplitude. The frequency variations of carrier wave depend upon the instantaneous amplitude of the signal as shown in Fig-1.

When the signal voltage is zero as at A, C, E and G, the carrier frequency is unchanged. When the signal approaches its positive peaks as at Band F, the carrier frequency is increased to maximum as shown by the closely spaced cycles. However, during the negative peaks of signal as at D, the carrier frequency is reduced to minimum as shown by the widely spaced cycles.

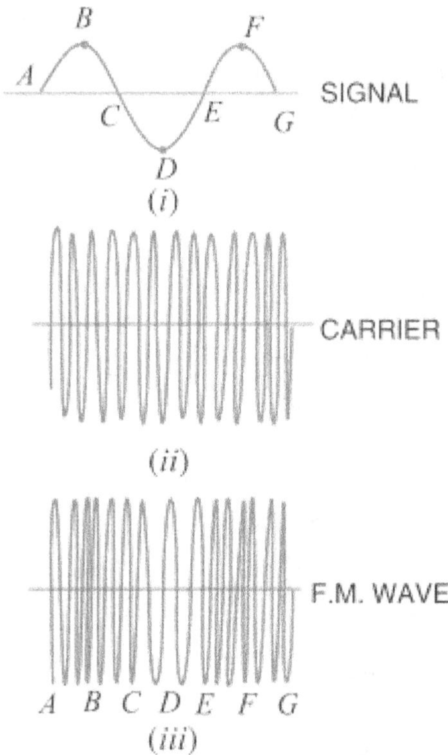

The process of frequency modulation (FM) can be made more illustrative if we consider numerical values. Fig. shows the FM signal having carrier frequency fc = 100 kHz. Note that FM signal has constant amplitude but varying frequencies above and below the carrier frequency of

100 kHz (= fc). For this reason, fc (= 100 kHz) is called centre frequency. The changes in the carrier frequency are produced by the audio-modulating signal. The amount of change in frequency from fc (= 100 kHz) or frequency deviation depends upon the amplitude of the audio-modulating signal. The frequency deviation increases with the increase in the modulating signal and vice versa. Thus the peak audio voltage will produce maximum frequency deviation. Referring to Fig. 16.13, the centre frequency is 100 kHz and the maximum frequency deviation is 30 kHz.

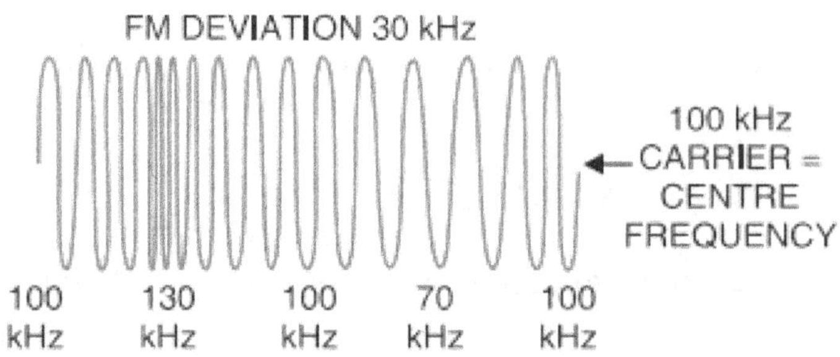

The following points about frequency modulation (FM) may be noted carefully :

(a) The frequency deviation of FM signal depends on the amplitude of the modulating signal.

(b) The centre frequency is the frequency without modulation or when the modulating voltage is zero.

(c) The audio frequency (i.e.frequency of modulating signal) does not determine frequency deviation.

SIMPLIFIED FM GENERATOR

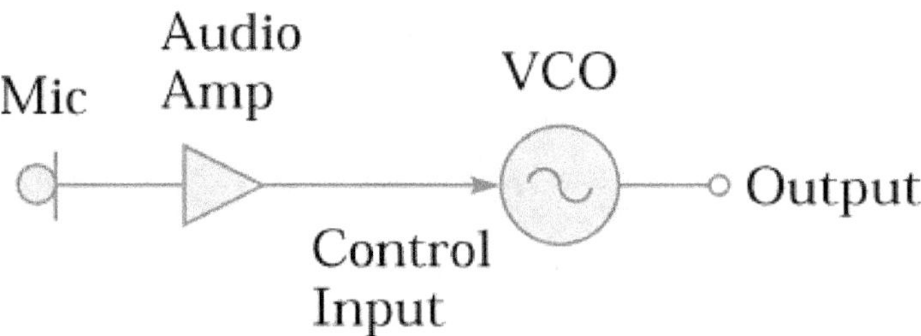

ADVANTAGES OF FM OVER AM

i.   It gives noiseless reception. Noise is a form of amplitude variations and a FM receiver will reject such signals.
ii. The operating range is quite large.
iii. It gives high-fidelity reception.
iv. The efficiency of transmission is very high.

4.2 THEORY OF FM

Suppose a modulating sine-wave signal $e_s(= E_s \cos \omega_s t)$ is used to vary the carrier frequency f_c. Let the change in carrier frequency be ke_s where, k is a constant known as the frequency deviation constant. The instantaneous carrier frequency f_i is given by

$$f_i = f_c + k\,e_s$$
$$= f_c + k\,E_s \cos \omega_s t$$

The factor kE_s represents the maximum frequency deviation and is denoted by Δf

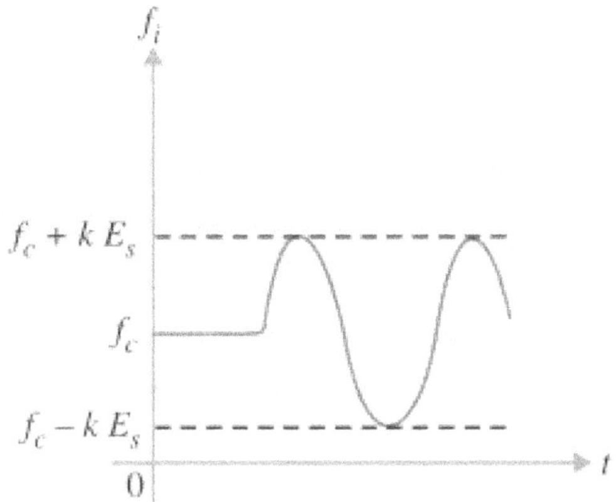

Fig: Frequency deviation

The instantaneous angular frequency of FM is given by

$$\omega_i = \omega_c + \Delta\omega_c \cos \omega_s t$$

Total phase angle $\theta = \omega t$ so that if ω is variable, then,

$$\theta = \int_0^t \omega_i \, dt$$

$$= \int_0^t (\omega_c + \Delta\omega_c \cos \omega_s t)\, dt$$

$$\therefore \qquad \theta = \omega_c t + \frac{\Delta\omega_c}{\omega_s} \sin \omega_s t$$

The term $\dfrac{\Delta\omega_c}{\omega_s}$ is called *modulation index* m_f.

$$\therefore \qquad \theta = \omega_c t + m_f \sin \omega_s t$$

The instantaneous value of FM voltage wave is given by ;

$$e = E_c \cos \theta$$

or

$$e = E_c \cos (\omega_c t + m_f \sin \omega_s t)$$

Which is the general voltage equation of a FM wave. The following points may be noted carefully:

(*i*) The modulation index m_f is the ratio of maximum frequency deviation (Δf) to the frequency ($= f_s$) of the modulating signal *i.e.*

$$\text{Modulation index, } m_f = \frac{\Delta\omega_c}{\omega_s} = \frac{f_{c\,(max)} - f_c}{f_s} = \frac{\Delta f}{f_s}$$

(*ii*) Unlike amplitude modulation, the modulation index (m_f) for frequency modulation can be greater than unity.

Where,

$$m_f = modulation\ index = \frac{\Delta f}{f_m} = \frac{k_f A_m}{f_m}$$

The difference between FM modulated frequency (instantaneous frequency) and normal carrier frequency is termed as Frequency Deviation. It is denoted by Δf, which is equal to the product of k_f and A_m

FM can be divided into Narrowband FM and Wideband FM based on the values of modulation index m_f

4.3 NARROWBAND FM

Following are the features of Narrowband FM.

i. This frequency modulation has a small bandwidth when compared to wideband FM.
ii. The modulation index m_f is small, i.e., less than 1.
iii. Its spectrum consists of the carrier, the upper sideband and the lower sideband.
iv. This is used in mobile communications such as police wireless, ambulances, taxicabs, etc.

4.4 WIDEBAND FM

Following are the features of Wideband FM.

i. This frequency modulation has infinite bandwidth.
ii. The modulation index m_f is large, i.e., higher than 1.
iii. Its spectrum consists of a carrier and infinite number of sidebands, which are located around it.
iv. This is used in entertainment, broadcasting applications such as FM radio, TV, etc.

4.5 FREQUENCY SPECTRUM

It requires advanced mathematics to derive the spectrum of FM wave. We will give only the results without derivation. If fc and fs are the carrier and signal frequencies respectively, then FM spectrum will have the following frequencies:

$$f_c \quad : \quad f_c \pm f_s \quad : \quad f_c \pm 2f_s \quad : \quad f_c \pm 3f_s \quad \text{and so on.}$$

Note that $f_c + f_s$, $f_c + 2f_s$, $f_c + 3f_s$ ...... are the upper sideband frequencies while $f_c - f_s$, $f_c - 2f_s$, $f_c - 3f_s$ ...... are the lower sideband frequencies.

4.6 BANDWIDTH

For FM, the bandwidth varies with both deviation and modulating frequency. Increasing modulating frequency reduces modulation index so it reduces the number of sidebands with significant amplitude. On the other hand, increasing modulating frequency increases the frequency separation between sidebands, Bandwidth increases with modulation frequency but is not directly proportional to it.

4.7 CARSON'S RULE

Carson's Rule provides an adequate approximation for determining FM signal bandwidth:

$$B = 2\left(\delta_{max} + f_{m(max)}\right)$$

Problem-4.1: A frequency modulated voltage wave is given by the equation:

$$e = 12 \cos\left(6 \times 10^8 t + 5 \sin 1250\, t\right)$$

Find

i. *carrier frequency*
ii. *signal frequency*
iii. *modulation index*
iv. *maximum frequency deviation*
v. *power dissipated by the FM wave in 10-ohm resistor.*

Solution. The given FM voltage wave is

$$e = 12 \cos (6 \times 10^8 t + 5 \sin 1250\, t)$$

The equation of standard FM voltage wave is

$$e = E_c \cos (\omega_c t + m_f \sin \omega_s t)$$

Comparing eqs. (i) and (ii), we have,

$$(i) \qquad \text{Carrier frequency}, f_c = \frac{\omega_c}{2\pi} = \frac{6 \times 10^8}{2\pi} = 95.5 \times 10^6 \text{ Hz}$$

$$(ii) \qquad \text{Signal frequency}, f_s = \frac{\omega_s}{2\pi} = \frac{1250}{2\pi} = 199 \text{ Hz}$$

$$(iii) \qquad \text{Modulation index}, m_f = 5$$

$$(iv) \qquad \text{Max. frequency deviation}, \Delta f = m_f \times f_s = 5 \times 199 = 995 \text{ Hz}$$

$$(v) \qquad \text{Power dissipated}, P = \frac{E_{r.m.s.}^2}{R} = \frac{(12/\sqrt{2})^2}{10} = 7.2\text{W}$$

Problem-4.2: *A 25 MHz carrier is modulated by a 400 Hz audio sine wave. If the carrier voltage is 4V and the maximum frequency deviation is 10 kHz, write down the voltage equation of the FM wave.*

Solution. The voltage equation of the FM wave is

$$e = E_c \cos (\omega_c t + m_f \sin \omega_s t)$$

$$\omega_c = 2\pi f_c = 2\pi \times 25 \times 10^6 = 1.57 \times 10^8 \text{ rad/s}$$

$$\omega_s = 2\pi f_s = 2\pi \times 400 = 2513 \text{ rad/s}$$

$$m_f = \frac{\Delta f}{f_s} = \frac{10 \text{ kHz}}{400 \text{ Hz}} = \frac{10 \times 10^3 \text{ Hz}}{400 \text{Hz}} = 25$$

$$e = 4 \cos (1.57 \times 10^8\, t + 25 \sin 2513 t) \quad \textbf{Ans.}$$

Problem-4.3: *Calculate the modulation index for an FM wave where the maximum frequency deviation is 50 kHz and the modulating frequency is 5 kHz.*

Solution.

$$\text{Max. frequency deviation}, \Delta f = 50 \text{ kHz}$$

$$\text{Modulating frequency}, f_s = 5 \text{ kHz}$$

$$\therefore \qquad \text{Modulation index}, m_f = \frac{\Delta f}{f_s} = \frac{50 \text{ kHz}}{5 \text{ kHz}} = 10$$

Problem-4.4: *The carrier frequency in an FM modulator is 1000 kHz. If the modulating frequency is 15 kHz, what are the first three upper sideband and lower sideband frequencies?*

Solution.

$$\text{Carrier frequency, } f_c = 1000 \text{ kHz}$$
$$\text{Modulating frequency, } f_s = 15 \text{ kHz}$$

Upper sideband frequencies

$f_c + f_s$	;	$f_c + 2f_s$	;	$f_c + 3f_s$
$1000 + 15$	;	$1000 + 2 \times 15$	;	$1000 + 3 \times 15$
1015 kHz	;	1030 kHz	;	1045 kHz

Lower sideband frequencies

$f_c - f_s$	;	$f_c - 2f_s$	;	$f_c - 3f_s$
$1000 - 15$	;	$1000 - 2 \times 15$	;	$1000 - 3 \times 15$
985 kHz	;	970 kHz	;	955 kHz

Problem-4.5: The carrier and modulating frequencies of an FM transmitter are 100 MHz and 15 kHz respectively. If the maximum frequency deviation is 75 kHz, find the bandwidth of FM signal.

Solution:

To calculate the exact bandwidth of an FM signal, it requires the use of advanced mathematics (Bessel functions) which is beyond the level of this book. However, the bandwidth of an FM signal is approximately given by;

$$\text{Bandwidth, } BW = 2\,[\,\Delta f + f_s\,] = 2\,[75 + 15] = 180 \text{ kHz}$$

Problem-4.6: In a frequency modulated wave, frequency deviation constant is 75 kHz/volt and the signal amplitude is 2V. Find the maximum frequency deviation.

Solution.

$$\text{Frequency deviation constant, } k = 75 \text{ kHz/V}$$
$$\text{Amplitude of signal, } E_s = 2V$$
$$\therefore \quad \text{Max. frequency deviation, } \Delta f = k\,E_s = 75 \times 2 = 150 \text{ kHz}$$

4.8 FM AND NOISE

One of the original reasons for developing FM was to give improved performance in the presence of noise, which is still one of the major advantages over AM. One way to approach the problem of FM and noise is think of noise as a phasor of random amplitude and phase angle

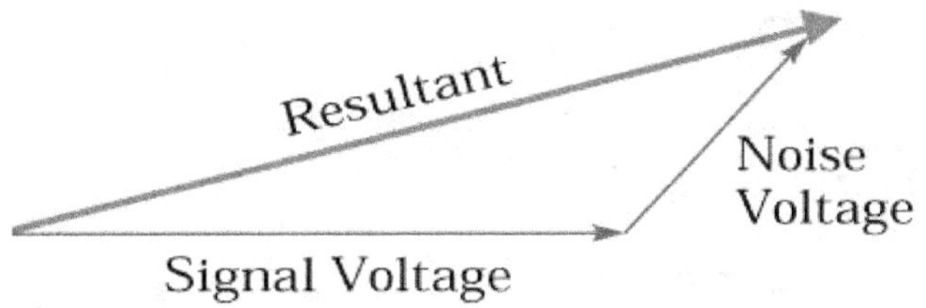

Fig: FM and Noise

4.9 FM NOISE LIMITER

The amplitude component of noise is easily dealt with in a well-designed FM system. Since FM signals do not depend on an envelope for detection, the receiver can employ limiting to remove any amplitude variations from the signal. A limiter may be considered as an amplifier whose output amplitude is clipped to a fixed value for a wide variety of input signal levels.

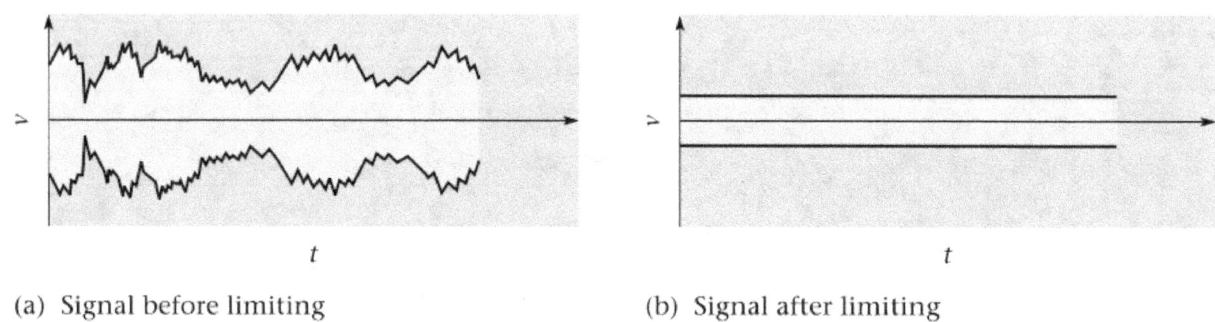

(a) Signal before limiting   (b) Signal after limiting

Fig: FM noise limiter

4.10 COMPARISON OF FM AND AM

FM	AM
The amplitude of carrier remains constant with modulation.	The amplitude of carrier changes with modulation.
The carrier frequency changes with modulation.	The carrier frequency remains constant with modulation.
The carrier frequency changes according to the strength of the modulating signal.	The carrier amplitude changes according to the strength of the modulating signal.
The value of modulation index can be more than 1.	The value of modulation factor cannot be more than 1 for distortionless AM signal.
FM system is complex	AM broadcasting is simpler than FM
FM doesn't degrade linearly with distance.	AM is more prone to signal distortion and degradation compared to FM
FM can transmit in stereo making it ideal for music.	AM usually broadcasts in mono which makes it sufficient for talk radio.
FM has a shorter range than AM	AM has a longer range than FM

4.11 FM MODULATOR

4.11.1 GENERATION OF NBFM:

We know that the standard equation of FM wave is

$$s(t) = A_c \cos\left(2\pi f_c t + 2\pi k_f \int m(t)\, dt\right)$$

$$\Rightarrow s(t) = A_c \cos(2\pi f_c t)\cos(2\pi k_f \int m(t)\, dt) -$$

$$A_c \sin(2\pi f_c t)\sin(2\pi k_f \int m(t)\, dt)$$

For NBFM,

$$\left|2\pi k_f \int m(t)\, dt\right| << 1$$

We know that $\cos\theta \approx 1$ and $\sin\theta \approx 1$ when θ is very small.

By using the above relations, we will get the NBFM equation as

$$s(t) = A_c \cos(2\pi f_c t) - A_c \sin(2\pi f_c t) 2\pi k_f \int m(t)\, dt$$

The block diagram of NBFM modulator is shown in the following figure 7.

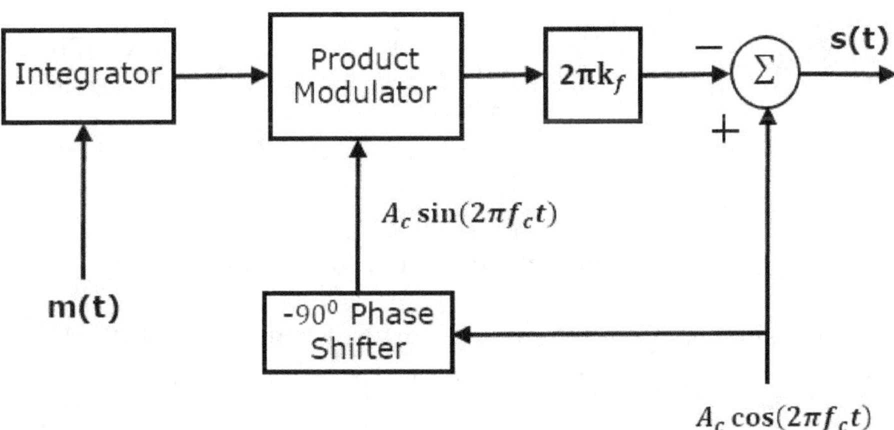

Fig-7: NBFM Generation

Here, the integrator is used to integrate the modulating signal $m(t)$. The carrier signal $A_c\cos(2\pi f_c t)$ is the phase shifted by -90_0 to get $A_c\sin(2\pi f_c t)$ with the help of -90_0 phase shifter. The product modulator has two inputs $\int m(t)dt$ and $A_c\sin(2\pi f_c t)$. It produces an output, which is the product of these two inputs.

This is further multiplied with $2\pi k_f$ by placing a block $2\pi k_f$ in the forward path. The summer block has two inputs, which are nothing but the two terms of NBFM equation. Positive and negative signs are assigned for the carrier signal and the other term at the input of the summer block. Finally, the summer block produces NBFM wave.

4.11.2 GENERATION OF WBFM:

The following two methods generate WBFM wave.

1. Direct method
2. Indirect method

4.11.2.1 DIRECT METHOD:

This method is called as the Direct Method because we are generating a wide band FM wave directly. In this method, Voltage Controlled Oscillator (VCO) is used to generate WBFM. VCO produces an output signal, whose frequency is proportional to the input signal voltage. This is similar to the definition of FM wave. The block diagram of the generation of WBFM wave is shown in the following figure.

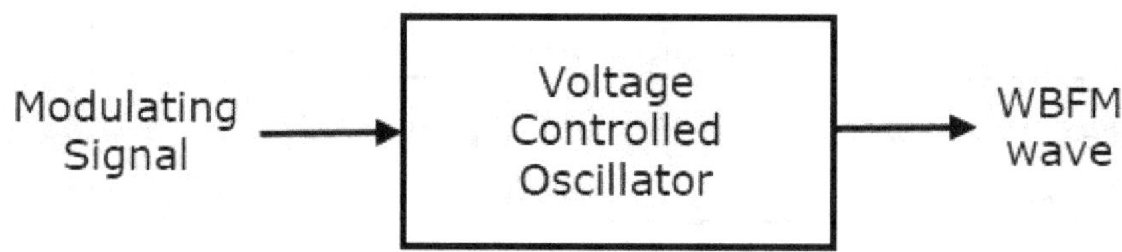

Fig: Direct method of WBFM generation

Here, the modulating signal $m(t)$ is applied as an input of Voltage Controlled Oscillator (VCO). VCO produces an output, which is nothing but the WBFM.

$$f_i \; \alpha \; m\,(t)$$

$$\Rightarrow f_i = f_c + k_f m\,(t)$$

Where, f_i is the instantaneous frequency of WBFM wave.

4.11.2.2 Indirect Method:

This method is called as Indirect Method because we are generating a wide band FM wave indirectly. This means, first we will generate NBFM wave and then with the help of frequency multipliers we will get WBFM wave. The block diagram of generation of WBFM wave is shown in the following figure.

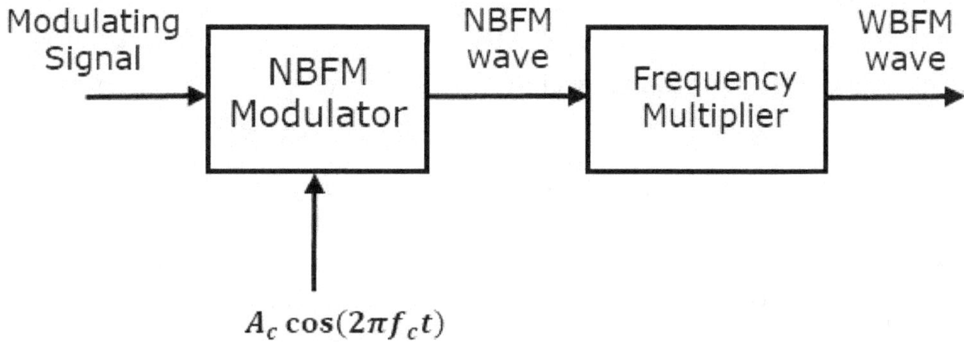

$$A_c \cos(2\pi f_c t)$$

Fig: Indirect method of WBFM

This block diagram contains mainly two stages. In the first stage, the NBFM wave will be generated using NBFM modulator. We have seen the block diagram of NBFM modulator at the beginning of this chapter. We know that the modulation index of NBFM wave is less than one. Hence, in order to get the required modulation index (greater than one) of FM wave, choose the frequency multiplier value properly.

Frequency multiplier is a non-linear device, which produces an output signal whose frequency is 'n' times the input signal frequency. Where, 'n' is the multiplication factor.

If NBFM wave whose modulation index β is less than 1 is applied as the input of frequency multiplier, then the frequency multiplier produces an output signal, whose modulation index is 'n' times β and the frequency also 'n' times the frequency of WBFM wave.

Sometimes, we may require multiple stages of frequency multiplier and mixers in order to increase the frequency deviation and modulation index of FM wave.

4.12 FM Demodulator

In this chapter, let us discuss about the demodulators which demodulate the FM wave. The following two methods demodulate FM wave.

1) Frequency discrimination method

2) Phase discrimination method

4.12.1 FREQUENCY DISCRIMINATION METHOD:

We know that the equation of FM wave is

$$s\left(t\right) = A_c \cos\left(2\pi f_c t + 2\pi k_f \int m\left(t\right) dt\right)$$

Differentiate the above equation with respect to 't'.

$$\frac{ds\left(t\right)}{dt} = -A_c\left(2\pi f_c + 2\pi k_f m\left(t\right)\right)\sin\left(2\pi f_c t + 2\pi k_f \int m\left(t\right) dt\right)$$

We can write, $-\sin\theta$ as $\sin\left(\theta - 180^0\right)$.

$$\Rightarrow \frac{ds(t)}{dt} = A_c\left(2\pi f_c + 2\pi k_f m\left(t\right)\right)\sin\left(2\pi f_c t + 2\pi k_f \int m\left(t\right) dt - 180^0\right)$$

$$\Rightarrow \frac{ds(t)}{dt} = A_c\left(2\pi f_c\right)\left[1 + \left(\frac{k_f}{k_c}\right) m\left(t\right)\right]\sin$$

$$\left(2\pi f_c t + 2\pi k_f \int m\left(t\right) dt - 180^0\right)$$

In the above equation, the amplitude term resembles the envelope of AM wave and the angle term resembles the angle of FM wave. Here, our requirement is the modulating signal $m(t)$. Hence, we can recover it from the envelope of AM wave.

The following figure 10 shows the block diagram of FM demodulator using frequency discrimination method.

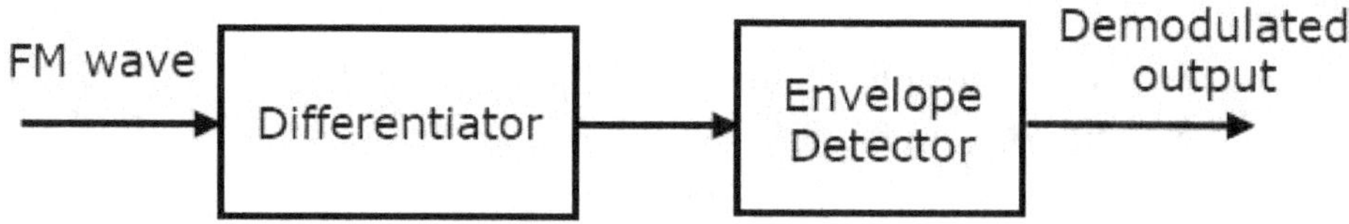

Fig: Frequency discrimination method

This block diagram consists of the differentiator and the envelope detector. Differentiator is used to convert the FM wave into a combination of AM wave and FM wave. This means, it converts the frequency variations of FM wave into the corresponding voltage (amplitude) variations of

AM wave. We know the operation of the envelope detector. It produces the demodulated output of AM wave, which is nothing but the modulating signal.

4.12.2 PHASE DISCRIMINATION METHOD:

The following figure shows the block diagram of FM demodulator using phase discrimination method.

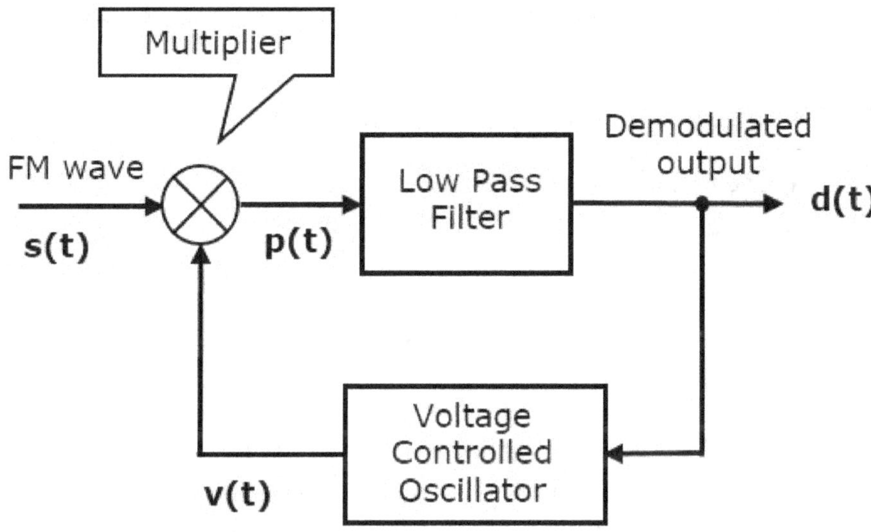

Fig: Phase discrimination method

This block diagram consists of the multiplier, the low pass filter, and the Voltage Controlled Oscillator (VCO). VCO produces an output signal $v(t)$, whose frequency is proportional to the input signal voltage $d(t)$. Initially, when the signal $d(t)$ is zero, adjust the VCO to produce an output signal $v(t)$, having a carrier frequency and −900 phase shift with respect to the carrier signal.

FM wave $s(t)$ and the VCO output $v(t)$ are applied as inputs of the multiplier. The multiplier produces an output, having a high frequency component and a low frequency component. Low pass filter eliminates the high frequency component and produces only the low frequency component as its output.

This low frequency component contains only the term-related phase difference. Hence, we get the modulating signal $m(t)$ from this output of the low pass filter.

4.13 FM IS NOISELESS. EXPLAIN IT

There is no change in amplitude with modulation in FM. So, we can say that FM has no envelope. Moreover FM receiver does not have to respond to amplitude variations. This lets it ignore noise to some extent.

4.14 Capture effect

The tendency of FM receiver to receive the strongest signal and reject others is called capture effect.

4.15 Splatter

- Frequency components that fall outside its assigned channel
- Produced by transmitter

CHAPTER-5
PHASE MODULATION

5.1 PHASE MODULATION

In frequency modulation, the frequency of the carrier varies. Whereas, in Phase Modulation (PM), the phase of the carrier signal varies in accordance with the instantaneous amplitude of the modulating signal.

So, in phase modulation, the amplitude and the frequency of the carrier signal remains constant. This can be better understood by observing the following figure.

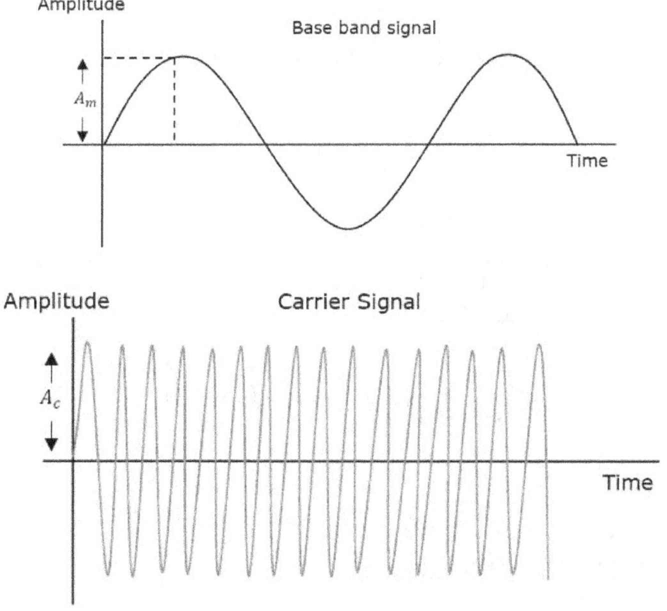

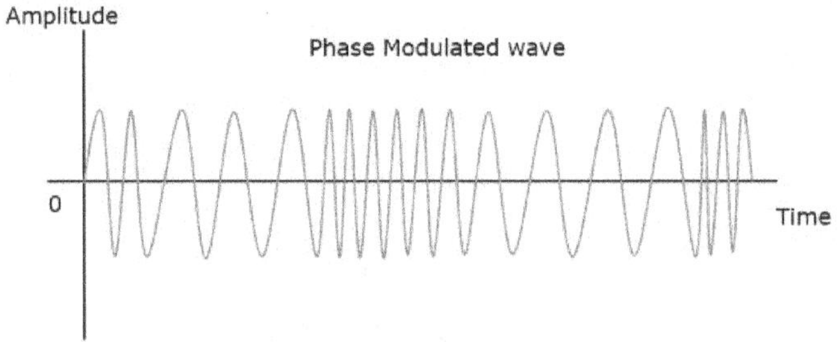

Fig: Phase Modulation

The phase of the modulated wave has got infinite points, where the phase shift in a wave can take place. The instantaneous amplitude of the modulating signal changes the phase of the carrier signal. When the amplitude is positive, the phase changes in one direction and if the amplitude is negative, the phase changes in the opposite direction.

Mathematical Representation of PM

The equation for instantaneous phase ϕ_i in phase modulation is

$$\phi_i = k_p m(t)$$

Where, k_p is the phase sensitivity, $m(t)$ is the message signal

The standard equation of angle modulated wave is

$$s(t) = A_c \cos(2\pi f_c t + \phi_i)$$

Substitute, ϕ_i value in the above equation

$$s(t) = A_c \cos(2\pi f_c t + k_p m(t))$$

This is the equation of PM wave.

If the modulating signal, $m(t) = A_m \cos(2\pi f_m t)$,

Then the equation of PM wave will be

$$s(t) = A_c \cos(2\pi f_c t + \beta \cos(2\pi f_m t))$$

Where, β = modulation index = $\Delta\phi = k_p A_m$, $\Delta\phi$ is phase deviation

In phase modulation, the phase shift is proportional to the instantaneous amplitude of the modulating signal. Phase modulation is used in mobile communication systems, while frequency modulation is used mainly for FM broadcasting.

5.2 DIFFERENCE BETWEEN FM AND PM

FM	PM
Frequency deviation is proportional to modulating signal m(t)	Phase deviation is proportional to modulating signal m(t)
Noise immunity is superior to PM (and of course AM)	Noise immunity better than AM but not FM
Signal-to-noise ratio (SNR) is better than in PM	Signal-to-noise ratio (SNR) is not as good as in FM
FM is widely used for commercial broadcast radio (88 MHz to 108 MHz)	PM is primarily for some mobile radio services
Modulation index is proportional to modulating signal m(t) as well as modulating frequency f_m	Modulation index is proportional to modulating signal m(t)

CHAPTER-6
ANALOG PULSE MODULATION

6.1 PULSE MODULATION

In Pulse modulation, a periodic sequence of rectangular pulses, is used as a carrier wave. This is further divided into analog and digital modulation.

6.1.1   Analog Modulation:

In analog modulation technique, if the amplitude or duration or position of a pulse is varied in accordance with the instantaneous values of the baseband modulating signal, then such a technique is called as Pulse Amplitude Modulation (PAM) or Pulse Duration/Width Modulation (PDM/PWM), or Pulse Position Modulation (PPM).

6.1.2   Digital Modulation:

In digital modulation, the modulation technique used is Pulse Code Modulation (PCM) where the analog signal is converted into digital form of 1s and 0s. As the resultant is a coded pulse train, this is called as PCM. This is further developed as Delta Modulation (DM). These digital modulation techniques will be discussed in 3rd year 2nd semester, course titled Digital Communication, ICT-605.

6.2 ANALOG PULSE MODULATION

1)   Pulse Amplitude Modulation (PAM)

2) Pulse Width Modulation (PWM)
3) Pulse Position Modulation (PPM)

6.2.1 PULSE AMPLITUDE MODULATION (PAM)

In Pulse Amplitude Modulation (PAM) technique, the amplitude of the pulse carrier varies, which is proportional to the instantaneous amplitude of the message signal.

The pulse amplitude modulated signal will follow the amplitude of the original signal, as the signal traces out the path of the whole wave. In natural PAM, a signal sampled at Nyquist rate can be reconstructed, by passing it through an efficient Low Pass Filter (LPF) with exact cutoff frequency.

Figure explains the Pulse Amplitude Modulation.

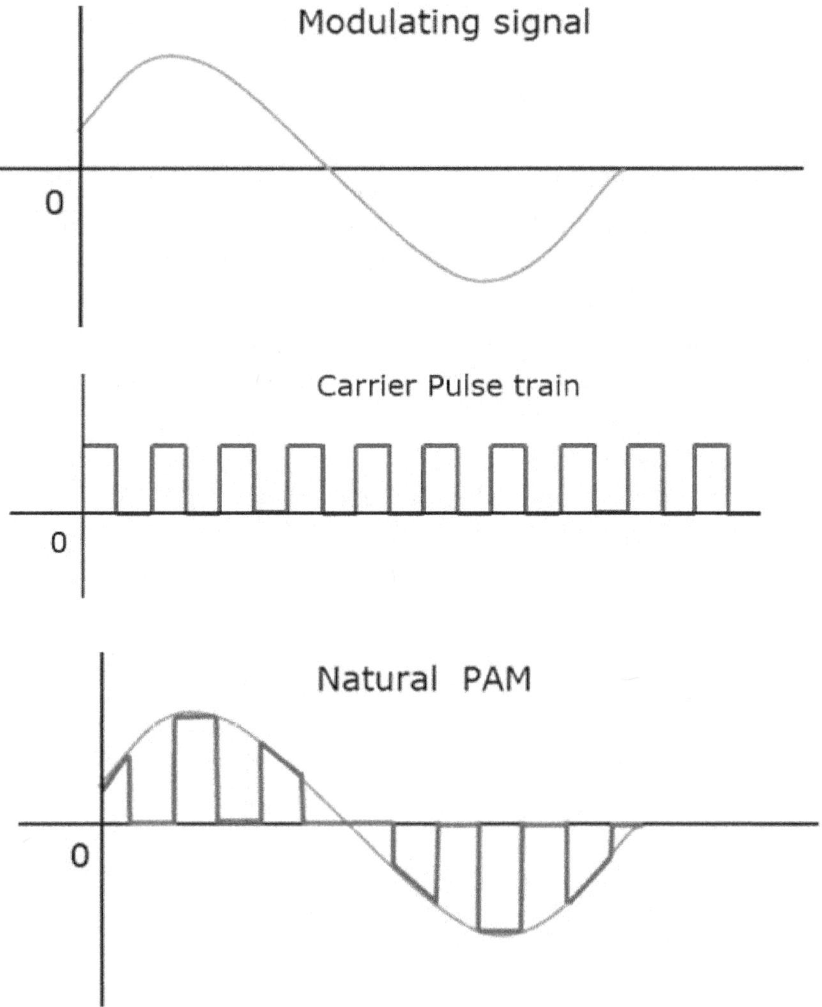

Fig: Pulse Amplitude Modulation

Though the PAM signal is passed through a LPF, it cannot recover the signal without distortion. Hence, to avoid this noise, use flat-top sampling. The flat-top PAM signal is shown in the following figure.

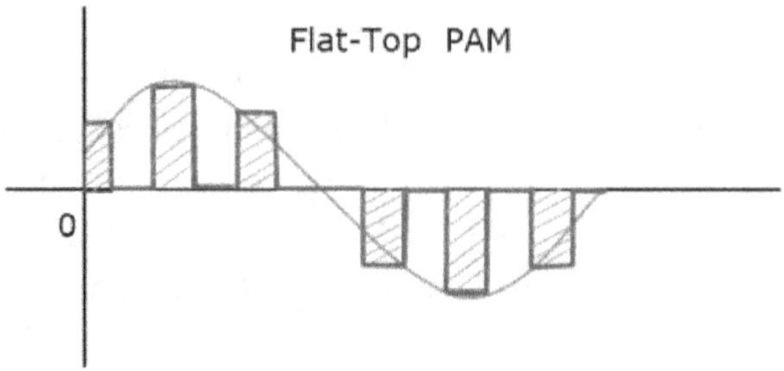

Fig: Flat top PAM signal

Flat-top sampling is the process in which, the sampled signal can be represented in pulses for which the amplitude of the signal cannot be changed with respect to the analog signal, to be sampled. The tops of amplitude remain flat. This process simplifies the circuit design.

6.2.2 PULSE WIDTH MODULATION

In Pulse Width Modulation (PWM) or Pulse Duration Modulation (PDM) or Pulse Time Modulation (PTM) technique, the width or the duration or the time of the pulse carrier varies, which is proportional to the instantaneous amplitude of the message signal.

The width of the pulse varies in this method, but the amplitude of the signal remains constant. Amplitude limiters are used to make the amplitude of the signal constant. These circuits clip off the amplitude to a desired level, and hence the noise is limited.

Figure explains the types of Pulse Width Modulations.

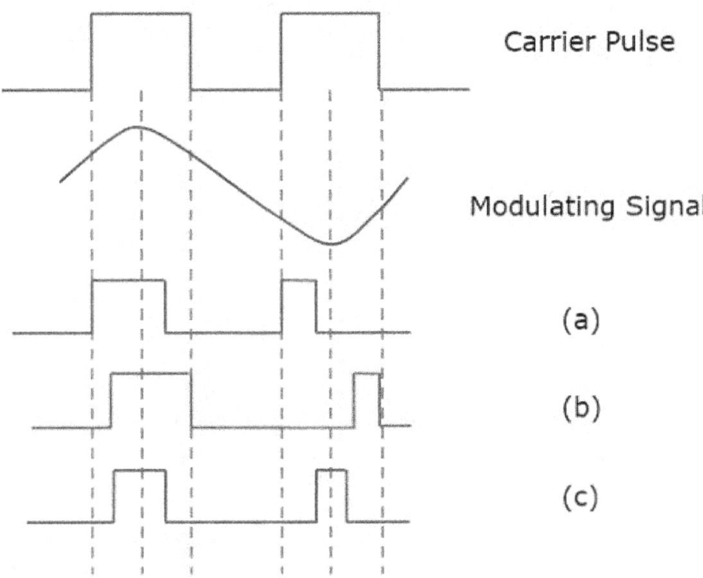

Fig: Pulse Width Modulation

There are three types of PWM.

1) The leading edge of the pulse being constant, the trailing edge varies according to the message signal. The waveform for this type of PWM is denoted as (a) in the above figure.
2) The trailing edge of the pulse being constant, the leading edge varies according to the message signal. The waveform for this type of PWM is denoted as (b) in the above figure.
3) The center of the pulse being constant, the leading edge and the trailing edge varies according to the message signal. The waveform for this type of PWM is denoted as (c) shown in the above figure.

6.2.3 PULSE POSITION MODULATION

Pulse Position Modulation (PPM) is an analog modulation scheme in which, the amplitude and the width of the pulses are kept constant, while the position of each pulse, with reference to the position of a reference pulse varies according to the instantaneous sampled value of the message signal.

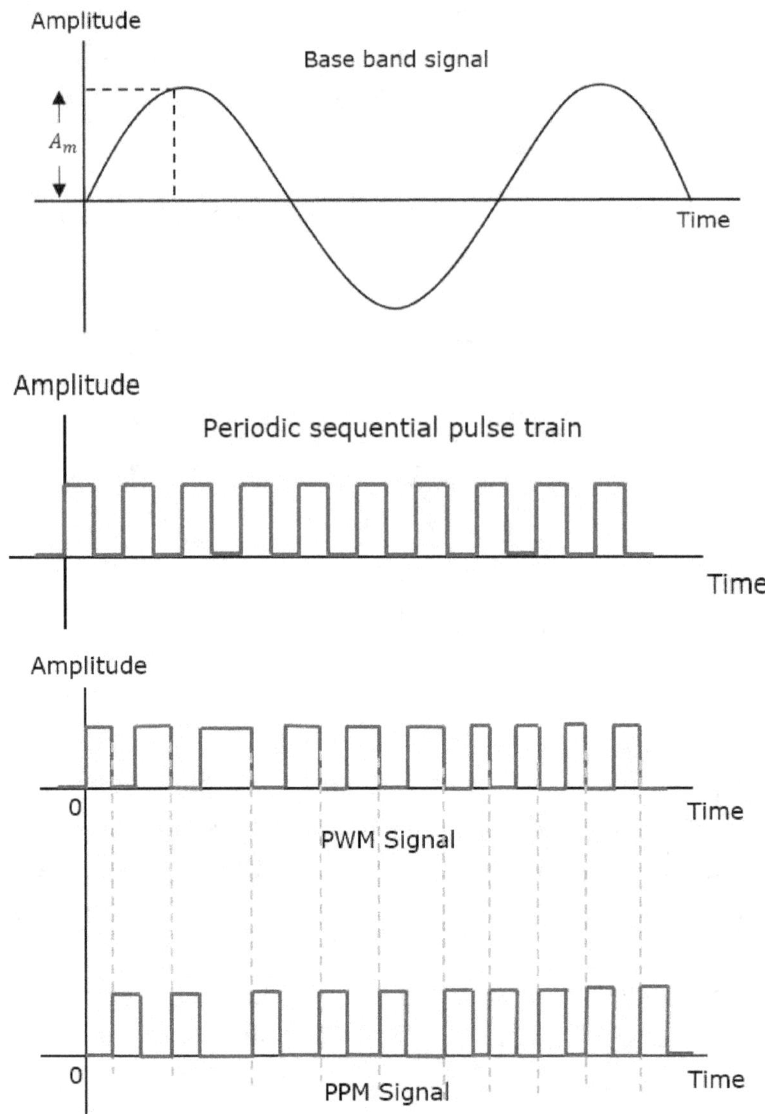

Fig: Pulse Position Modulation

The transmitter has to send synchronizing pulses (or simply sync pulses) to keep the transmitter and the receiver in sync. These sync pulses help to maintain the position of the pulses. The following figures explain the Pulse Position Modulation.

Pulse position modulation is done in accordance with the pulse width modulated signal. Each trailing edge of the pulse width modulated signal becomes the starting point for pulses in PPM signal. Hence, the position of these pulses is proportional to the width of the PWM pulses.

Advantage

As the amplitude and the width are constant, the power handled is also constant.

Disadvantage

The synchronization between the transmitter and the receiver is a must.

6.3 COMPARISON BETWEEN PAM, PWM, AND PPM

The following table presents the comparison between three modulation techniques.

PAM	PWM	PPM
Amplitude is varied	Width is varied	Position is varied
Bandwidth depends on the width of the pulse	Bandwidth depends on the rise time of the pulse	Bandwidth depends on the rise time of the pulse
Instantaneous transmitter power varies with the amplitude of the pulses	Instantaneous transmitter power varies with the amplitude and the width of the pulses	Instantaneous transmitter power remains constant with the width of the pulses
System complexity is high	System complexity is low	System complexity is low
Noise interference is high	Noise interference is low	Noise interference is low
It is similar to amplitude modulation	It is similar to frequency modulation	It is similar to phase modulation

CHAPTER-7

RADIO TRANSMITTER

7.1 WHAT IS RADIO TRANSMITTER?

A radio transmitter is an electronic device which, when connected to an antenna, produces an electromagnetic signal.

The function of a transmitter is to generate a modulated signal with sufficient power, at the right frequency, and to couple that signal into an antenna feed line.

7.2 APPLICATIONS OF RADIO TRANSMITTER

- ➢ Radio and television broadcasting
- ➢ Two way communications or radar.
- ➢ Remote control

7.3 TRANSMITTER DESIGN REQUIREMENTS

A transmitter must generate a signal with the following criteria:

1. Frequency Accuracy and Stability:

The accuracy and stability of the transmitter is fixed by the carrier oscillator. Exact requirements are determined by the application of the transmitter and by regulatory agencies.

2. Frequency Agility:

Frequency agility is the ability to change operating frequency rapidly, without extensive retuning. Broadcast transmitters are rarely retuned. Other services, such as CB, require rapid and accurate retuning to other channels.

3. Spectral Purity:

Spectral purity is a measure of the spurious signals generated by a transmitter. All transmitters generate frequencies other than the carrier and the sidebands required for the modulation scheme in use. All frequencies except the assigned transmitting frequency must be filtered out to avoid interference with other transmissions

4. Power Output:

There are a number of ways to measure transmitter power, depending upon the modulation scheme employed. Transmitters for full-carrier AM are rated in terms of carrier power. Suppressed-carrier AM transmitters are rated by peak-envelope power (PEP). FM transmitters are rated by total power output.

5. Efficiency:

There are two important reasons for efficient transmitter operation:

- ➢ Most obvious is energy conservation

➢ Power that enters the transmitter but does not exit via the transmitter output is converted into heat
➢ Large amounts of heat require significant amounts of additional hardware to remove the heat, adding to the cost of the equipment

6. Modulation Fidelity:

An ideal communication system allows the original information signal to be recovered exactly, except for a time delay. Compression is often used to raise the overall modulation level of the signal. Compression distorts the overall dynamic range of the original signal, but results in an improved signal-to-noise ratio. Other types of distortion such as inter-modulation and harmonic distortion must also be kept at a minimum.

7.4 AM TRANSMITTER

AM transmitter takes the audio signal as an input and delivers amplitude modulated wave to the antenna as an output to be transmitted. The block diagram of AM transmitter is shown in the following figure.

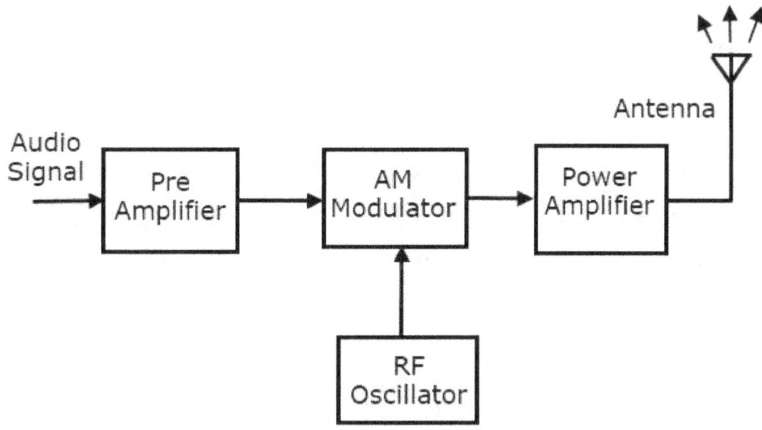

Fig: AM Transmitter

The working of AM transmitter can be explained as follows.

1. **Pre-amplifier:** The audio signal from the output of the microphone is sent to the pre-amplifier, which boosts the level of the modulating signal.
2. **RF Oscillator:** The RF oscillator generates the carrier signal.
3. **AM Modulator:** Both the modulating and the carrier signal is sent to AM modulator.
4. **Power Amplifier:** Power amplifier is used to increase the power levels of AM wave. This wave is finally passed to the antenna to be transmitted.

7.5 FM TRANSMITTER

FM transmitter is the whole unit, which takes the audio signal as an input and delivers FM wave to the antenna as an output to be transmitted. The block diagram of FM transmitter is shown in the following figure.

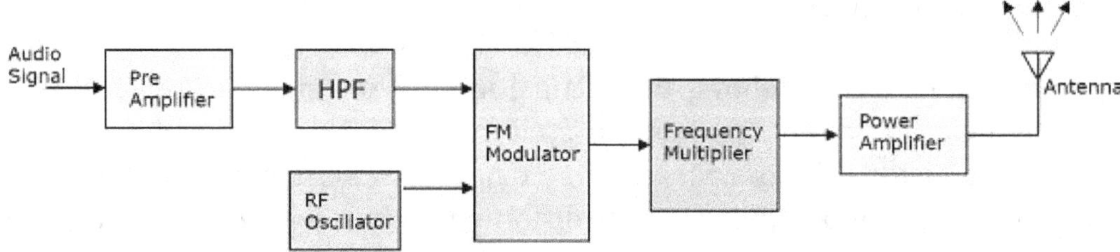

Fig: FM Transmitter

The working of FM transmitter can be explained as follows.

1. **Pre-amplifier:** The audio signal from the output of the microphone is sent to the pre-amplifier, which boosts the level of the modulating signal.
2. **High Pass Filter:** This signal is then passed to high pass filter, which acts as a pre-emphasis network to filter out the noise and improve the signal to noise ratio.
3. **FM Modulator:** This signal is further passed to the FM modulator circuit.
4. **RF Oscillator:** The oscillator circuit generates a high frequency carrier, which is sent to the modulator along with the modulating signal.
5. **Frequency Multiplier:** Several stages of frequency multiplier are used to increase the operating frequency. Even then, the power of the signal is not enough to transmit.
6. **Power Amplifier:** Hence, a RF power amplifier is used at the end to increase the power of the modulated signal. This FM modulated output is finally passed to the antenna to be transmitted.

7.6 TRANSMITTER TOPOLOGY

The figure at the right shows the block diagrams of some typical transmitters. There are many varieties of transmitters but most are based upon these structures.

7.6.1 High level modulation (AM)

In Figure which represents a typical transmitter for full-carrier AM. The carrier is generated by a frequency synthesizer and amplified to its full output power before modulation takes place. The optional frequency multiplier would be used if the required carrier frequency were higher than could be conveniently generated by the synthesizer.

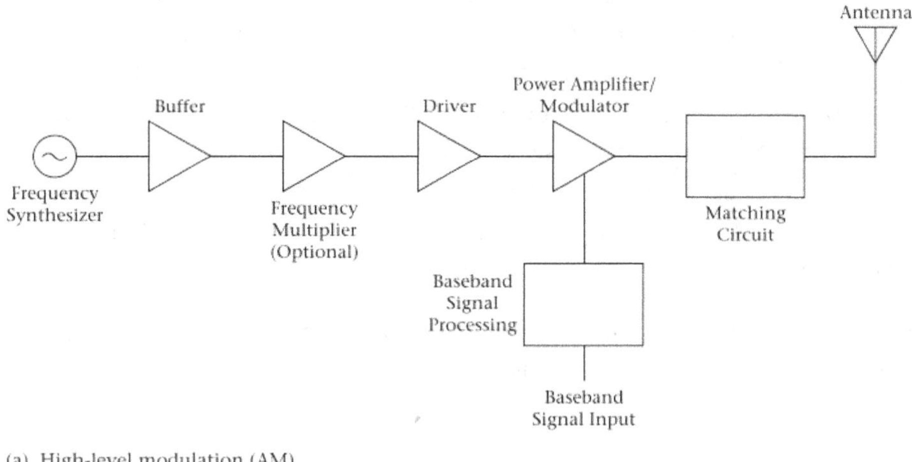

Fig: High level modulation (AM)

By delaying modulation as long as possible, this topology allows all the RF amplifier stages in the transmitter to operate in a nonlinear mode for greater efficiency. High-power AM modulators are relatively easy to build, so this is the preferred topology for AM.

7.6.2 Low level modulation of synthesizer (FM and FSK)

When the modulation involves changing the transmitted frequency as in FM and FSK, it is usual to modulate the carrier oscillator. In the example shown in Figure, that oscillator is a frequency synthesizer. The optional frequency multiplier would multiply the frequency deviation as well as the carrier frequency, which makes it useful in case the modulated oscillator cannot achieve the required deviation.

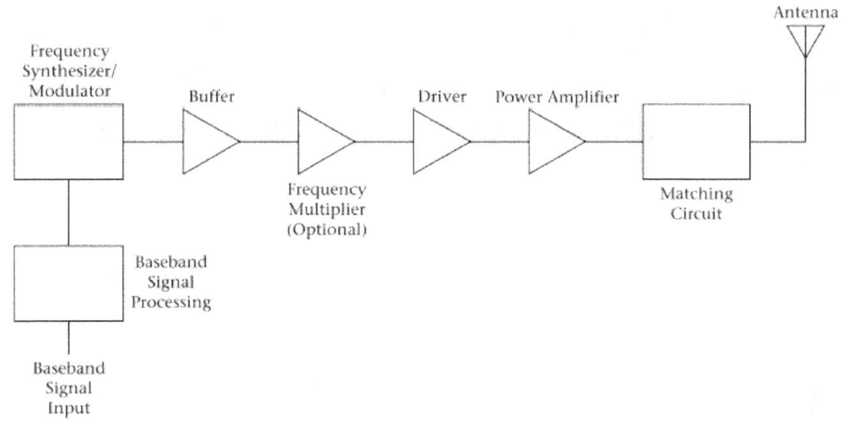

Fig: Low level modulation of Synthesizer (FM, FSK)

7.6.3 Heterodyne system

Figure shows a slightly more complex design, generally used where it is more convenient to modulate the signal at a fixed frequency. The modulated signal is then moved to the required output frequency by an oscillator-mixer combination, with the oscillator usually taking the form of a frequency synthesizer. A band pass filter eliminates undesired mixing components and sends the signal to an amplifier chain. All three transmitter designs end with a multistage amplifier. Two stages are shown: the driver and power amplifier. More may be required, especially for high output power levels. The matching circuit matches the power amplifier to the antenna feed line impedance, which is usually 50 Ω, and also removes harmonics and other spurious signals from the transmitter output.

The power amplifier must be linear for any signal that has variable amplitude unless, as with Figure 3, the modulation is done at the transmitter output.

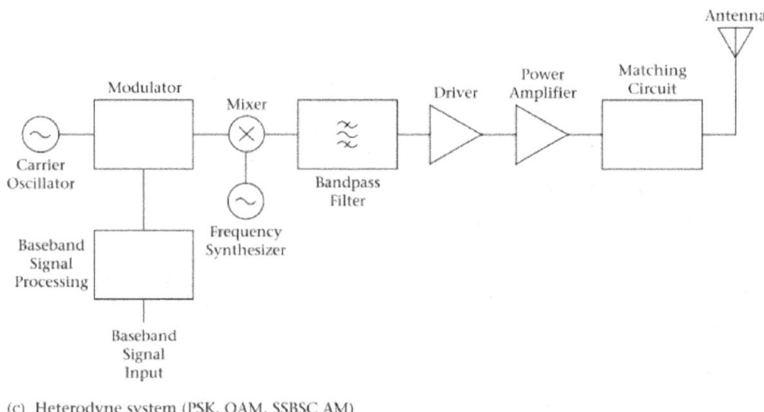

(c) Heterodyne system (PSK, QAM, SSBSC AM)

Fig: Heterodyne System (PSK, QAM, SSBSC AM)

7.7 FREQUENCY SYNTHESIZER

Figure shows how a simple frequency synthesizer works. A phase locked loop controls the frequency of a voltage-controlled oscillator so that it is always a multiple of a crystal-controlled reference frequency.

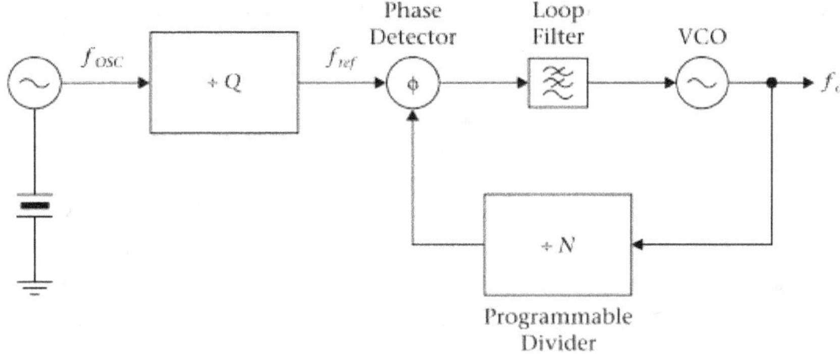

Fig: Frequency Synthesizer

$$f_o = Nf_{ref}$$

where

$$f_o = \text{output frequency}$$
$$f_{ref} = \text{reference frequency}$$
$$N = \text{divider modulus (must be an integer)}$$

By changing the modulus N of the programmable divider, the output frequency can be varied in steps equal to the reference frequency f_{ref}. Since f_{ref} must often be quite small (a few kilohertz), usually a fixed divider is used to reduce the frequency of a crystal oscillator to the required value.

Problem-7.1: Using a 25.6-MHz crystal for the reference oscillator, configure a frequency synthesizer to generate frequencies from 100 to 200 MHz at 10 0-kHz intervals.

SOLUTION

The step size is 100 kHz so let us use that value for f_{ref}. Then

$$Q = \frac{25.6 \times 10^6}{100 \times 10^3}$$

$$= 256$$

To find the range of values of N, look at the extremes of the frequency range. At the low end,

$$N = \frac{100 \times 10^6}{100 \times 10^3}$$

$$= 1000$$

Similarly, at the high end, $N = 2000$.

7.8 SINGLE-SIDEBAND SUPPRESSED CARRIER AM TRANSMITTERS

1. Balanced Modulators for Double-Sideband Suppressed-Carrier Generation:

Balanced modulators are used for DSSC generation. The output of a balanced modulator is shown here:

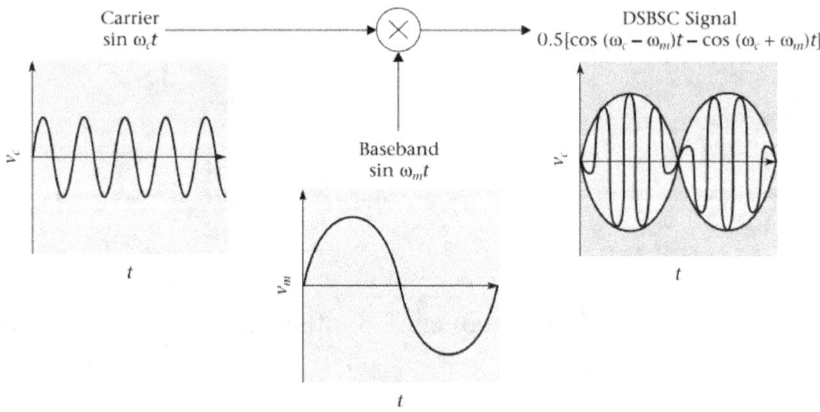

Fig: Single sideband AM transmitters

2. Single-Sideband Suppressed-Carrier AM:

Generating an SSB signal is much more complicated than for AM, and is nearly always done at low power and at only one frequency. The frequency is then shifted by mixing, as in Figure 8. The usual way to generate SSB is to first develop a double sideband suppressed-carrier signal (DSBSC) using a balanced modulator (otherwise known as a multiplier).

It can be shown that if the carrier and baseband signals are multiplied together the result will contain upper and lower sidebands but no carrier. Suppose that a carrier and a modulation signal, each sine waves with 1 V peak amplitude, are applied to a multiplier as shown in Figure 8.

The output of the multiplier will be

$$v_o = \sin \omega_m t \, \sin \omega_c t$$
$$= 0.5[\cos(\omega_c - \omega_m)t - \cos(\omega_c + \omega_m)t]$$

which is a DSBSC signal.

The DSBSC signal can be converted into SSB by using a band pass filter to pass the desired sideband while rejecting the other sideband. Figure 8 illustrates the idea.

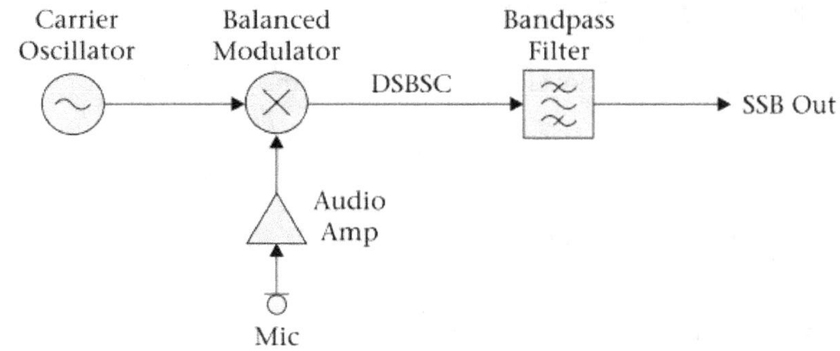

(a) Block diagram

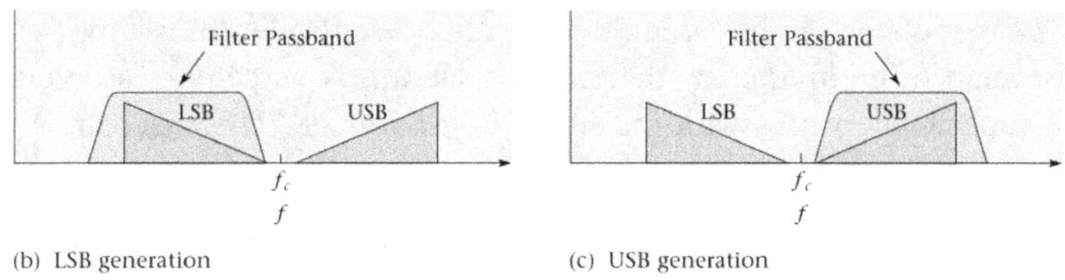

(b) LSB generation   (c) USB generation

Fig: SSBSC generation

Problem-7.2: An SSBSC generator of the type shown in Figure 9.5 has the following specifications:

Filter center frequency:	5.000 MHz
Filter bandwidth:	3 kHz
Carrier oscillator frequency:	4.9985 MHz

(a) Which sideband will be passed by the filter?

(b) What frequency should the carrier oscillator have if it is required to generate the other side band?

SOLUTION

(a) Since the carrier frequency is at the low end of the filter pass band, the upper sideband will be passed.

(b) To generate the lower sideband, the carrier frequency should be moved to the high end of the filter pass band, at 5.0015 MHz

7.9 FM TRANSMITTERS TYPES

FM Transmitters typically use the following components and configurations:

1) Direct-FM Modulators
2) Frequency Multipliers
3) Phase-Locked Loop FM Generators
4) Indirect-FM Modulators
5) Digital FM Modulators

7.9.1 PLL FM MODULATOR

Any crystal or LC oscillator can be turned into a voltage-controlled oscillator (VCO) by using a varactor diode as part of the frequency determining circuit. A varactor is a reverse-biased diode whose junction capacitance varies with the applied bias voltage. The baseband signal modulates the bias voltage to generate FM.

Unfortunately, VCOs using crystal oscillators have a very small maximum frequency deviation and are able to operate at only one frequency (a significant drawback). On the other hand, LC oscillators tend to be unstable.

However, by making the modulated VCO part of a frequency synthesizer, it is possible to build a stable signal source whose frequency can be varied over a wide range. Figure shows how it can be done.

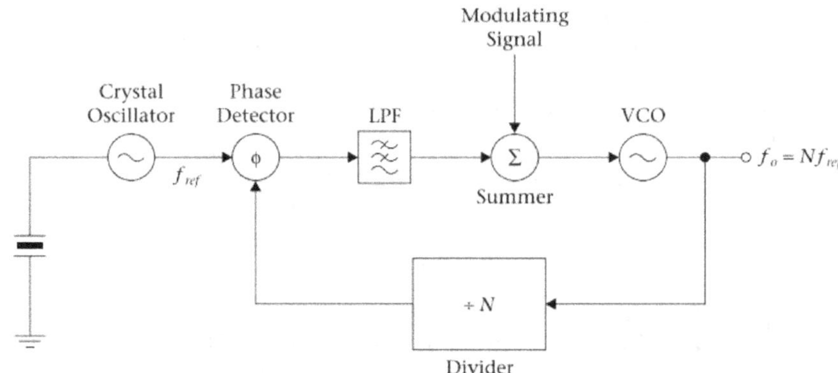

Fig: PLL FM Modulator

As in the frequency synthesizer described earlier, the carrier frequency is equal to Nf_{ref}. The baseband signal is added to the VCO control voltage from the phase detector. The change in VCO frequency due to modulation is detected by the phase detector, but the low-pass filter prevents the correction signal generated by the phase detector from reaching the VCO and canceling out the modulation. We thus have a combined frequency synthesizer and FM modulator. Most FM transmitters used for wireless communication use this scheme or a variation of it.

Problem-7.3: The power amplifier of an AM transmitter has an output carrier power of 25 W and an efficiency of 70%. How much power will have to be supplied to this stage for 100% modulation?

The power supply input to the modulator/amplifier stage –
$P_s = 25\ W\ /\ 0.7 = 35.7\ W$
So, required audio power –
$P_a = 0.5 P_s = 35.7\ /2 = 17.9\ W$. Ans.

Problem-7.4: If the transmitter in the previous question operates from a 24 V supply, what will be the impedance seen looking into the power amplifier from the modulation transformer secondary?

For m=100%, peak voltage at the modulation transformer secondary –
$V_p = Vcc = 24\ V$
$V_{rms} = V_p\ /\sqrt{2} = 17\ V.$

We know, $R_L = V^2\ /\ P$
Or, $Z_a = V_{rms}^2\ /\ P_a = 17\ V\ /\ 17.9\ W = 16.1\ \Omega$. Ans.

Problem-7.5: A transistor RF power amplifier is designed to produce 30 W output with a supply voltage of 50 V.
   (a) If the efficiency of the stage is 70%, what is the average collector current?
   (b) What is the impedance seen by the modulation transformer secondary?
   (c) What power output would be required from the audio stage for m=100%?
   (d) What is the maximum voltage that appears between the collector and emitter of the transistor?

(a) The DC supply system must supply power to the amplifier –
$P_{dc} = P_s = P_o\ /\eta = 30\ W\ /\ 0.7 = 42.9\ W$
The average current drawn from the power supply is given by
$P_{dc} = V_{cc} I_c$
Or, $I_c = P_{dc}\ /\ V_{cc} = 42.9\ W/\ 50\ V = 0.857\ A$

(b) The audio amplifier must supply audio power to the RF amplifier:
   $P_a = 0.5 P_s = 42.9\ W\ /\ 2 = 21.45\ W$
   The peak voltage at the secondary of the modulation transformer: $V_p = V_{cc};$
   or, RMS voltage at the secondary of the modulation transformer: $V_{rms} = V_{cc}\ /\ \sqrt{2} = 50\ /\sqrt{2}$
   $= 35.4\ V$
   The impedance seen by the transformer can be found from:
   $P = V^2\ /\ R;$
   Or, $R = Z_a = V_{rms}^2\ /\ P_a = 35.4\ V\ /\ 21.45\ W = 58.3\ \Omega.$
(c) The audio stage must supply 21.45 W.

(d) $V_{max} = 4V_{cc} = 4 \times 50 = 200$ V

OUTPUT IMPEDANCE MATCHING

The peak voltage of unmodulated output:

Vo(pk) = Vcc

Vo(rms) = Vcc/$\sqrt{2}$

$$R_L = \frac{\left(\dfrac{V_{cc}}{\sqrt{2}}\right)^2}{P_c} = \frac{V_{cc}^2}{2P_c}$$

Where, R_L = load resistance at the output of the device, P_C=carrier power output, without modulation, V_{cc}= supply voltage

Problem-7.6: The RF power amplifier of a transmitter produces 30 W output with a supply voltage of 50 V. Calculate the required load impedance for the amplifier.

Give, P_c = 30 W; V_{cc} = 50 V.

The required load resistance

$$R_L = V^2_{cc}/2P_c$$
$$= 50^2/2 \times 30$$
$$= 2500/60$$
$$= 41.67 \ \Omega. \text{ Ans.}$$

Chapter-8
Radio Receiver

8.1 What is Receiver?

The receiver performs an inverse function to that of the transmitter. It must separate the desired signal from others present at the antenna, amplify it and demodulate it to recover the original baseband signal.

8.2 Receiver Specifications

1. Sensitivity:

The ability to receive weak signals with an acceptable signal-to-noise ratio is called sensitivity. It is expressed in terms of the voltage or power at the antenna terminals necessary to achieve a specified signal-to-noise ratio or some more easily measured equivalent.

2. Selectivity:

The ability to discriminate against interfering signals is known as selectivity.

3. Adjacent channel rejection:

Adjacent channel rejection is another way of specifying selectivity that is commonly used with channelized systems. It is defined as the number of decibels by which an adjacent channel signal must be stronger than the desired signal for the same receiver output.

4. Alternate channel rejection:

Alternate channel rejection is also used in systems, such as FM broadcasting, where stations in the same locality are not assigned to adjacent channels. The alternate channel is two channels removed from the desired one. It is also known as the second adjacent channel.

5. Distortion:

Distortion comes in several forms:

- Harmonic distortion is when the frequencies generated are multiples of those in the original signal
- Intermodulation distortion occurs when frequency components in the original signal mix and produce sum and difference signals
- Phase distortion consists of irregular shifts in phase and is common when signals pass through filters

6. Dynamic Range:

The ratio between between the receiver's response to weak signals and signals that are overload one or more stages is referred to as Dynamic Range. Blocking may occur when two adjacent signals, one of which is much stronger than the other, cause a reduction in sensitivity to the desired channel. This is also referred to as desensitization or desense

7. Spurious Responses:

Superheterodyne receivers have a tendency to receive signals they are not tuned to. Image Frequencies are signals that are produced as a result of the generation of intermediate frequencies

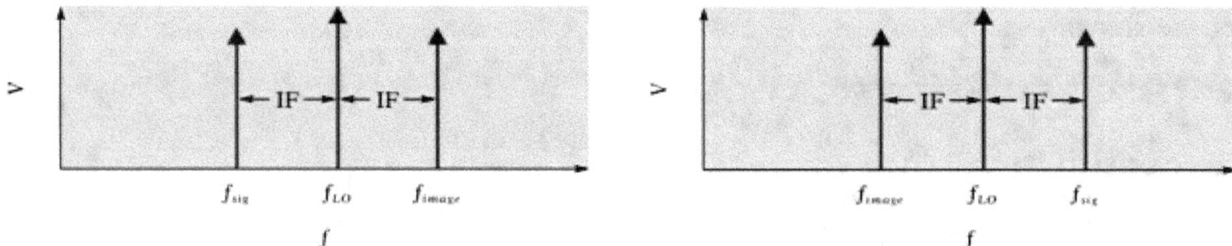

Fig: Spurious response

8.3 RF MIXING

The RF mixing unit develops an Intermediate Frequency (IF) to which any received signal is converted, so as to process the signal effectively.

RF Mixer is an important stage in the receiver. Two signals of different frequencies are taken where one signal level affects the level of the other signal, to produce the resultant mixed output. The input signals and the resultant mixer output is illustrated in the following figure.

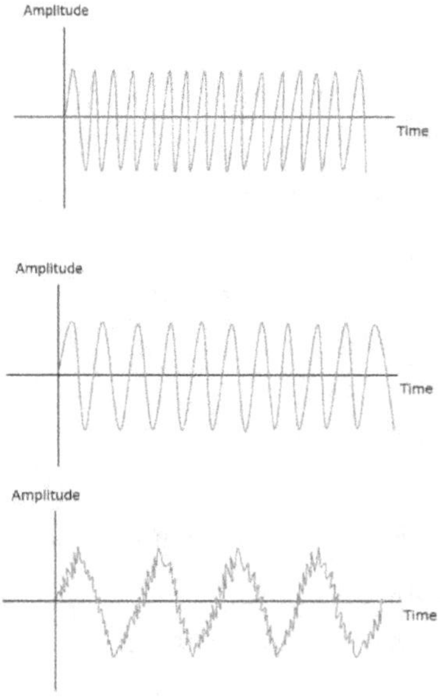

Fig: RF Mixing

Let the first and second signal frequencies be f_1 and f_2. If these two signals are applied as inputs of RF mixer, then it produces an output signal, having frequencies of f_1+f_2 and f_1-f_2.

If this is observed in the frequency domain, the pattern looks like the following figure.

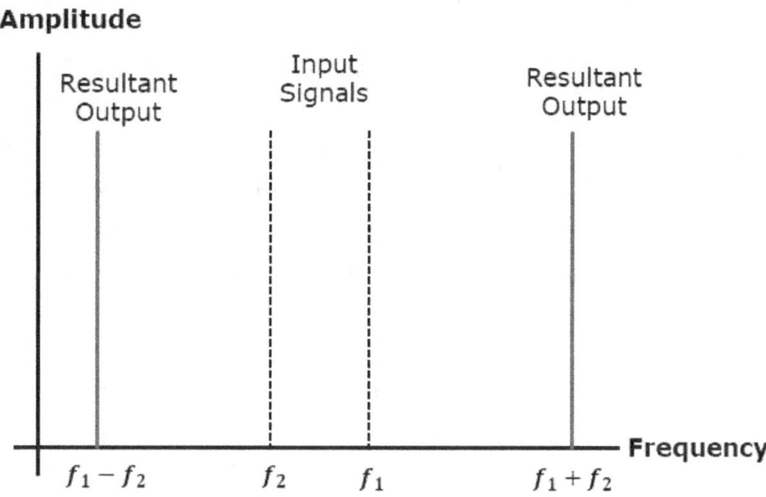

Fig: RF mixing in frequency domain

In this case, f_1 is greater than f_2. So, the resultant output has frequencies f_1+f_2 and f_1-f_2. Similarly, if f_2 is greater than f_1, then the resultant output will have the frequencies f_1+f_2 and f_1-f_2.

8.4 A.M. RADIO RECEIVERS

A radio receiver is a device which reproduces the modulated or radio waves into sound waves.

8.4.1 FUNCTIONS OF AM RECEIVERS

In order to reproduce the A.M. wave into sound waves, every radio receiver must perform the following functions:

i.   The receiving aerial must intercept a portion of the passing radio waves.
ii. The radio receiver must select the desired radio wave from a number of radio waves intercepted by the receiving aerial. For this purpose, tuned parallel LC circuits must be used. These circuits will select only that radio frequency which is in resonant with them.
iii. The selected radio wave must be amplified by the tuned frequency amplifiers.
iv. The audio signal must be recovered from the amplified radio wave.
v.   The audio signal must be amplified by suitable number of audio-amplifiers.
vi. The amplified audio signal should be fed to the speaker for sound reproduction.

8.4.2 Types of A.M. Radio Receivers

A.M. radio receivers can be broadly classified into two types viz., straight radio receiver and superhetrodyne radio receiver. The former was used in the early days of radio communication. However at present, all radio receivers are of superhetrodyne type.

8.4.2.1 Straight radio receiver

Figure shows the block diagram of a straight radio receiver. The aerial is receiving radio waves from different broadcasting stations. The desired radio wave is selected by the R.F. amplifier which employs a tuned parallel circuit. The selected radio wave is amplified by the tuned R.F. amplifiers. The amplified radio wave is fed to the detector circuit. This circuit extracts the audio signal from the radio wave. The output of the detector is the audio signal which is amplified by one or more stages of audio-amplification. The amplified audio signal is fed to the speaker for sound reproduction.

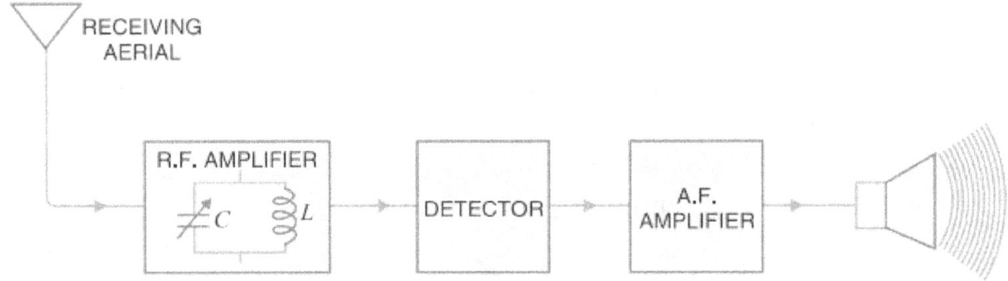

Fig: Straight Radio receiver

Limitations of straight radio receiver:

> - In straight radio receivers, tuned circuits are used. As it is necessary to change the value of variable capacitors (gang capacitors) for tuning to the desired station, therefore, there is a considerable variation of Q between the closed and open positions of the variable capacitors. This changes the sensitivity and selectivity of the radio receivers.
> - There is too much interference of adjacent stations.

8.4.2.2 Superhetrodyne Receiver

The shortcomings of straight radio receiver were overcome by the invention of superhetrodyne receiver by Major Edwin H. Armstrong during the First World War. At present, all modern receivers utilize the superhetrodyne circuit.

In this type of radio receiver, the selected radio frequency is converted to a fixed lower value, called intermediate frequency (IF). This is achieved by a special electronic circuit called mixer circuit.

There is a local oscillator in the radio receiver itself. This oscillator produces high frequency waves.

The selected radio frequency is mixed with the high frequency wave by the mixer circuit. In this process, beats are produced and the mixer produces a frequency equal to the difference between local oscillator and radio wave frequency.

The circuit is so designed that oscillator always produces a frequency 455 kHz above the selected radio frequency. Therefore, the mixer will always produce an intermediate frequency of 455 kHz regardless of the station to which the receiver is tuned. For instance, if 600 kHz station is tuned, then local oscillator will produce a frequency of 1055 kHz. Consequently, the output from the mixer will have a frequency of 455 kHz. Figure 5 shows the superhetrodyne principle with a block diagram. The selected radio frequency f1 is mixed with a frequency f2 from a local oscillator. The output from the mixer is a difference (i.e. f2– f1) and is always 455 kHz regardless of the station to which the receiver is tuned.

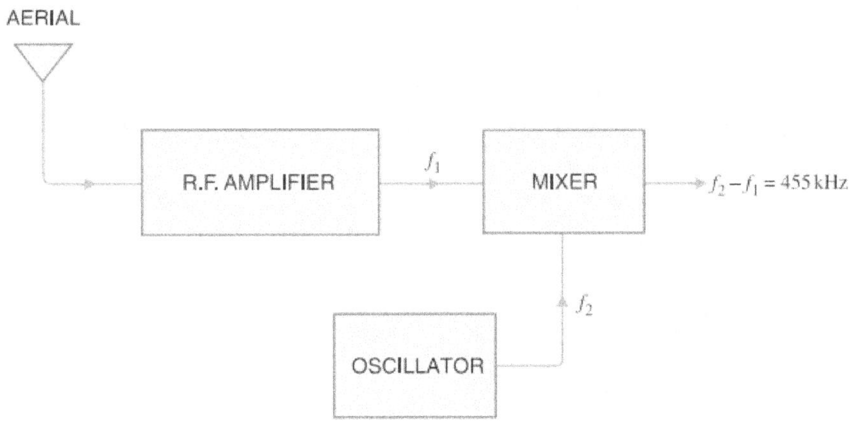

Fig: Superheterodyne principle

The production of fixed intermediate frequency (455 kHz) is the salient feature of superhetrodyne circuit. At this fixed intermediate frequency, the amplifier circuits operate with maximum stability, selectivity and sensitivity. As the conversion of incoming radio frequency to the intermediate frequency is achieved by heterodyning or beating the local oscillator against radio frequency, therefore, this circuit is called superhetrodyne circuit.

Stages of Superhetrodyne Radio Receiver:

Figure 6 shows the block diagram of a superhetrodyne receiver. It may be seen that R.F. amplifier stage, mixer stage and oscillator stage use tuned parallel circuits with variable capacitors. These capacitors are ganged together as shown by the dotted interconnecting lines. The rotation of the common shaft simultaneously changes the capacitance of these tuned circuits.

R.F. amplifier stage: The R.F. amplifier stage uses a tuned parallel circuit L1C1 with a variable capacitor C1. The radio waves from various broadcasting stations are intercepted by the receiving aerial and are coupled to this stage. This stage selects the desired radio wave and raises the strength of the wave to the desired level.

Mixer stage: The amplified output of R.F. amplifier is fed to the mixer stage where it is combined with the output of a local oscillator. The two frequencies beat together and produce an intermediate frequency (IF). The intermediate frequency is the difference between oscillator frequency and radio frequency i.e.

$$I.F. = Oscillator\ frequency - Radio\ frequency$$

The IF is always 455 kHz regardless of the frequency to which the receiver is tuned. The reason why the mixer will always produce 455 kHz frequency above the radio frequency is that oscillator always produces a frequency 455 kHz above the selected radio frequency. This is achieved by making C3 smaller than C1 and C2. By making C3 smaller, oscillator will tune to a higher frequency. In practice, capacitance of C3 is designed to tune the oscillator to a frequency higher than radio wave frequency by 455 kHz. This frequency difference (i.e. 455 kHz) will always be maintained because when C1 and C2 are varied, C3 will also vary proportionally. It may be noted that in mixer stage, the carrier frequency is reduced. The IF still contains the audio signal.

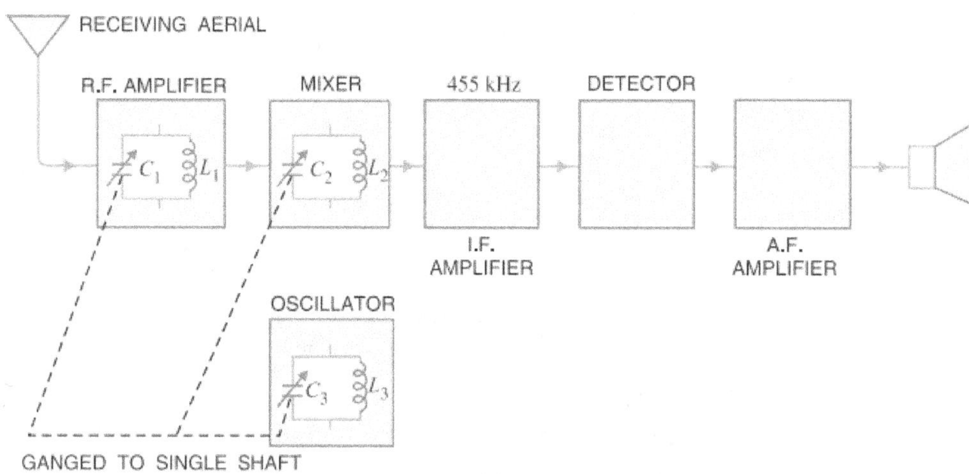

Fig: Superheterodyne receiver

I.F. amplifier stage: The output of mixer is always 455 kHz and is fed to fixed tuned I.F. amplifiers. These amplifiers are tuned to one frequency (i.e. 455 kHz) and render nice amplification.

Detector stage: The output from the last IF amplifier stage is coupled to the input of the detector stage. Here, the audio signal is extracted from the IF output. Usually, diode detector circuit is used because of its low distortion and excellent audio fidelity.

A.F. amplifier stage: The audio signal output of detector stage is fed to a multistage audio amplifier. Here, the signal is amplified until it is sufficiently strong to drive the speaker. The speaker converts the audio signal into sound waves corresponding to the original sound at the broadcasting station.

Advantages of Superhetrodyne Circuit

The basic principle involved in superhetrodyne circuit is to obtain a fixed intermediate frequency with the help of a mixer circuit and local oscillator. The superhetrodyne principle has the following advantages:

i. ***High R.F. amplification:*** The superhetrodyne principle makes it possible to produce an intermediate frequency (i.e. 455 kHz) which is much less than the radio frequency. R.F. amplification at low frequencies is more stable since feedback through stray and interelectrode capacitance is reduced.

ii. ***Improved selectivity:*** Losses in the tuned circuits are lower at intermediate frequency. Therefore, the quality factor Qof the tuned circuits is increased. This makes the amplifier circuits to operate with maximum selectivity.

iii. ***Lower cost:*** In a superhetrodyne circuit, a fixed intermediate frequency is obtained regardless of the radio wave selected. This permits the use of fixed R.F. amplifiers. The superhetrodyne receiver is thus cheaper than other radio receivers.

8.5 FM RECEIVER

The FM receiver is more complicated and, therefore, more expensive than the normal AM receiver. As we shall see, an FM receiver also uses superheterodyne principle. The FM broadcast signals lie in the frequency range between 88 MHz and 108 MHz. The IF (intermediate frequency) of an FM receiver is 10.7 MHz—much higher than the IF value of 455 kHz in AM receivers. Fig. 7 shows the block diagram of an FM receiver. In the interest of understanding, we shall discuss the various sections of the FM receiver.

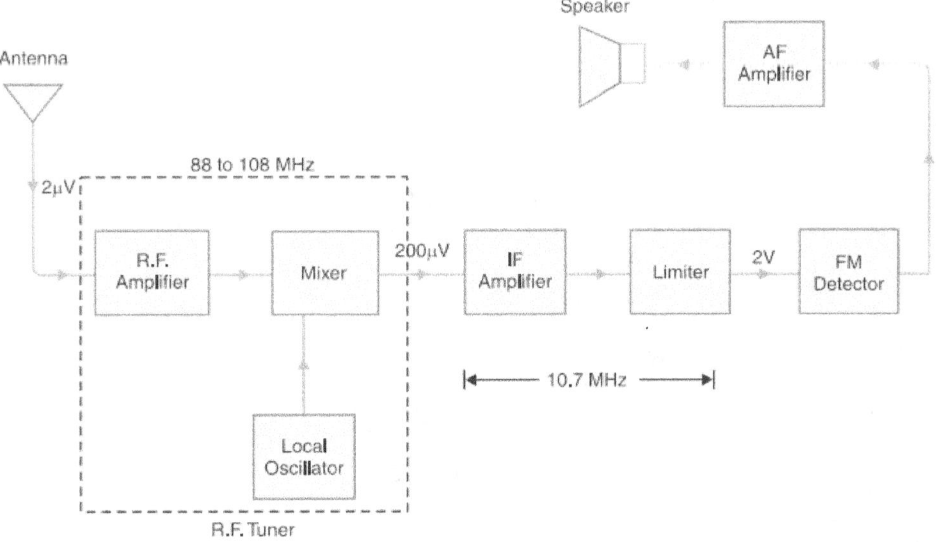

Fig: FM Receiver

R.F. Tuner:

The FM signals are in the frequency range of 88 to 108 MHz. The weak FM signal (say 2 μV) is picked up by the antenna and is fed to the R.F. tuner. The R.F. tuner consists of R.F. amplifier, Mixer and local oscillator.

The R.F. amplifier amplifies the selected FM signal (to 200 μV in the present case). The output from the RF amplifier is fed to the mixer stage where it is combined with the output signal from a local oscillator. The two frequencies beat together and produce an intermediate frequency (IF). The intermediate frequency (IF) is equal to the difference between oscillator frequency and the RF frequency. The IF is always 10.7 MHz (Recall IF in AM receiver is 455 kHz) regardless of the frequency to which the FM receiver is tuned.

IF Amplifier Stage:

The output signal from the mixer always has a frequency of 10.7 MHz and is fed to the IF amplifiers. Since IF amplifiers are tuned to IF (= 10.7 MHz), they render nice amplification. Note that bandwidth of IF amplifiers is about 200 kHz or 0.2 MHz. The IF gain is very large (assumed 10,000 in this case) so that output is 2V.

The IF is the difference between the incoming signal frequency and the local oscillator frequency. The local-oscillator frequency can be higher than the signal frequency, in which case the receiver is said to use high-side injection, or lower than the signal frequency (low-side injection).

For high-side injection, we need

$$f_{IF} = f_{LO} - f_{SIG}$$

so

$$f_{LO} = f_{SIG} + f_{IF}$$

where

$$f_{IF} = \text{intermediate frequency}$$
$$f_{LO} = \text{local-oscillator frequency}$$
$$f_{SIG} = \text{signal frequency}$$

Similarly, for low-side injection we need

$$f_{IF} = f_{SIG} - f_{LO}$$
$$f_{LO} = f_{SIG} - f_{IF}$$

Limiter Stage:

The output from IF stage is fed to the limiter. This circuit is an IF amplifier tuned to 10.7 MHz but its main function is to remove AM interference from the FM signal. Fig. 8 shows how the limiter removes AM interference from the FM signal. The input is an FM signal, but it has different amplitude levels because of AM interference has been added. However, the limiter circuit keeps the output level constant for different input levels.

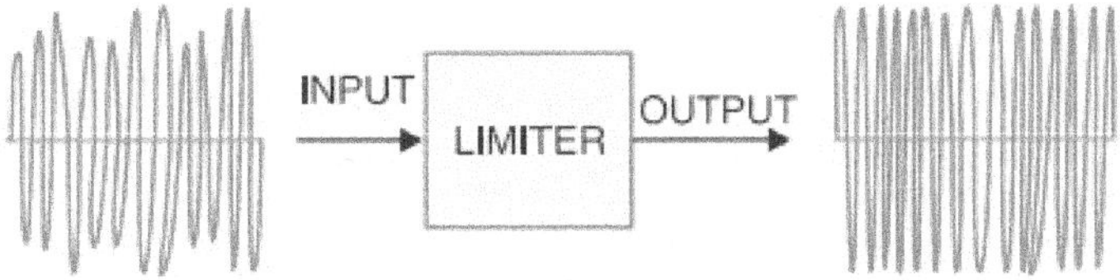

FM Detector:

After the removal of amplitude modulation from the FM signal by the limiter, the IF signal drives the input of the FM detector. An FM detector is a circuit that converts frequency variations to amplitude variations. The FM detector is also called a discriminator because it can distinguish between different frequencies in the input to provide different output voltages. The resultant amplitude modulated signal is then rectified and amplified for feeding to speaker for sound reproduction.

8.6 DIFFERENCE BETWEEN FM AND AM RECEIVERS

Both FM and AM receivers employ superheterodyne principle. However, the following are the points of differences between the two types of receivers:

i.   An FM receiver has two additional stages viz. limiter and discriminator, which are quite different from an AM receiver.
ii. FM broadcast signals lie in the frequency range between 88 and 108 MHz whereas AM broadcast signals lie in the frequency range from 540 kHz to 1600 kHz.
iii. FM receivers are free from interference and this means that much weaker signals can be successfully handled.
iv. FM bandwidth is about 200 kHz compared to 10 kHz bandwidth for AM.
v.   The IF for FM receivers is 10.7 MHz whereas IF for AM receivers is 455 kHz.

***Problem-8.1:** A receiver tunes from 500 MHz to 600 MHz with an IF of 20 MHz. Calculate the range of local-oscillator frequencies required if the receiver uses:*

(a) high-side injection (b) low-side injection

(a) For a signal frequency of 500 MHz we require

$$f_{LO} = f_{SIG} + f_{IF}$$
$$= 500 \text{ MHz} + 20 \text{ MHz}$$
$$= 520 \text{ MHz}$$

Similarly, a signal frequency of 600 MHz requires a local-oscillator frequency of 620 MHz.

(b) For a signal frequency of 500 MHz we need

$$f_{LO} = f_{SIG} - f_{IF}$$
$$= 500 \text{ MHz} - 20 \text{ MHz}$$
$$= 480 \text{ MHz}$$

Similarly, for a signal frequency of 600 MHz, the local oscillator must operate at 580 MHz.

Problem-8.2: A receiver has its local oscillator set to 550 MHz and its IF amplifier designed to work at 20 MHz. Find two signal frequencies that can be received.

Solution:

$$f_{IF} = f_{LO} - f_{SIG}$$

$$f_{SIG} = f_{LO} - f_{IF}$$
$$= 550 \text{ MHz} - 20 \text{ MHz}$$
$$= 530 \text{ MHz}$$

$$f_{IF} = f_{SIG} - f_{LO}$$
$$f_{SIG} = f_{LO} + f_{IF}$$
$$= 550 \text{ MHz} + 20 \text{ MHz}$$
$$= 570 \text{ MHz}$$

8.7 AM Demodulator

8.7.1 Full Carrier AM demodulator:

Full-carrier amplitude modulation can be demodulated with a very simple circuit

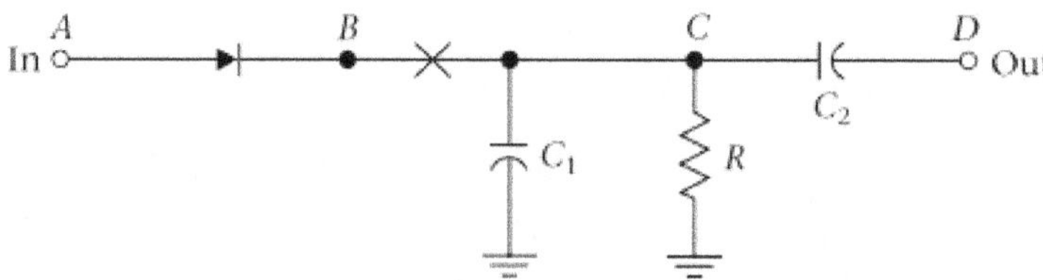

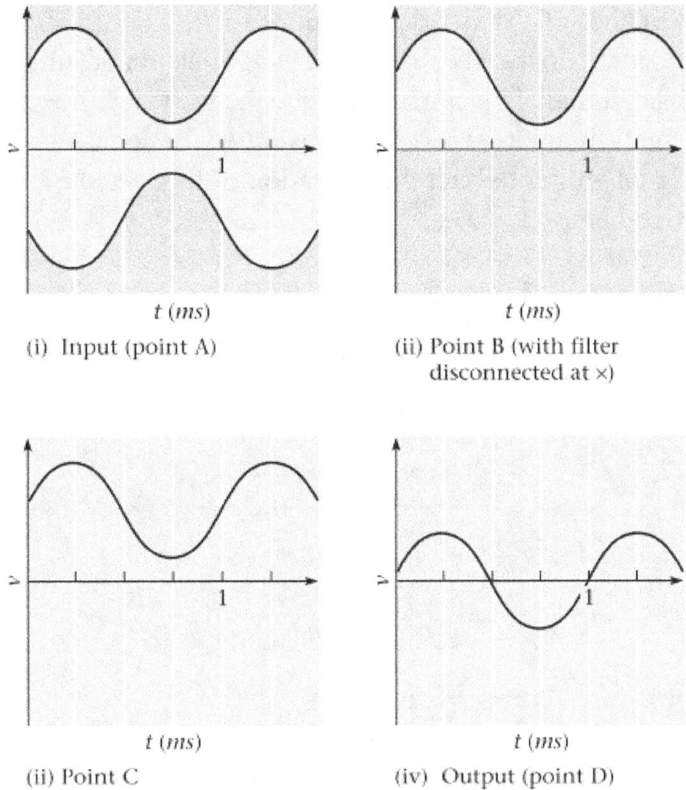

Fig: Full Carrier AM demodulator

All that is necessary to rectify the signal is to remove half of the envelope and then filter out the intermediate frequency component. A simple RC filter is sufficient for this.

8.8 FM Demodulators (Detectors)

There are four major types of FM detectors:

1. Foster-Seely discriminator
2. Ratio detector
3. Quadrature detector
4. PLL detector

8.8.1 PLL Method

The use of a phase-locked loop to demodulate FM signals is very straightforward.

The incoming FM signal is used to control the frequency of the VCO. As the incoming frequency varies, the PLL generates a control voltage to change the VCO frequency, which will follow that of the incoming signal. This control voltage varies at the same rate as the frequency of the incoming signal, thus it can be used directly as the output of the circuit.

Unlike the PLLs used in transmitter modulator circuits, this PLL must have a short time constant so that it can follow the modulation. The capture range of the PLL is not important, since the free-running frequency of the VCO will be set equal to the signal's carrier frequency at the detector (that is, to the center of the IF passband). The lock range must be at least twice the maximum deviation of the signal. If it is deliberately made wider, the detector will be able to function in spite of a small amount of receiver mistuning or local oscillator drift. Amplitude variations of the input signal will not affect the operation of this detector, unless they are so great that it stops working altogether.

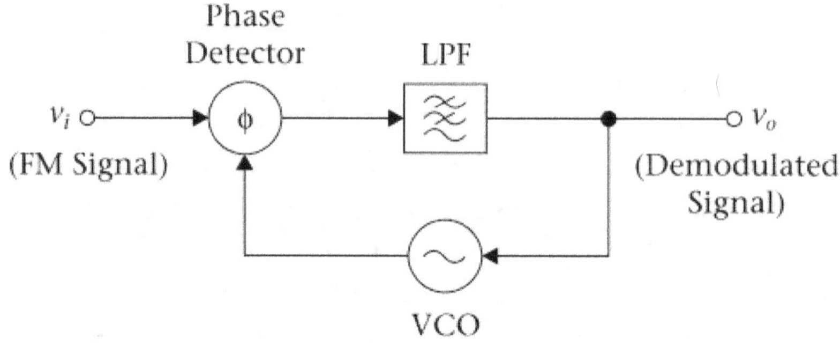

Fig: PLL FM Detector

8.8.2 QUADRATURE DETECTOR

Like the PLL detector, the quadrature detector is adapted to integrated circuitry.

In the quadrature detector (see Figure 11), the incoming signal is applied to one input of a phase detector. The signal is also applied to a phase-shift network. This consists of a capacitor (C1 in the figure) with high reactance at the carrier frequency, which causes a 90° phase shift (this is the origin of the term quadrature).

The tuned circuit consisting of L1 and C2 is resonant at the carrier frequency. Therefore, it causes no phase shift at the carrier frequency but does provide a phase shift at other frequencies that will add to or subtract from the basic 90° shift caused by C1.

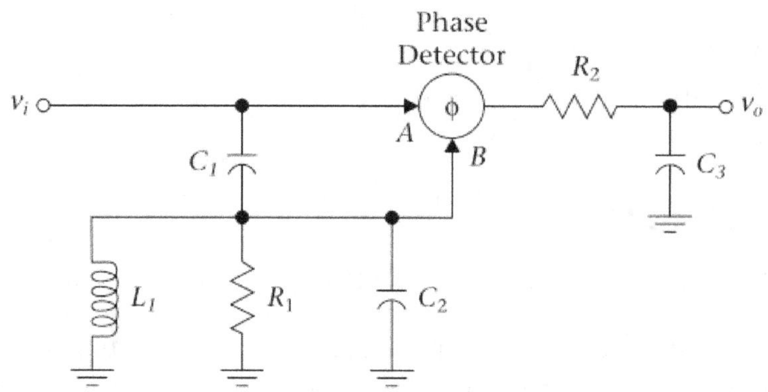

Fig: Quadrature FM Detector

The output of the phase-shift network is applied to the second input of the phase detector. When the input frequency changes, the angle of phase shift in the quadrature circuit varies, as the resonant circuit becomes inductive or capacitive. The output from the phase detector varies at the signal frequency but has an average value proportional to the amount the phase angle differs from 90°.

Low-pass filtering the output will recover the modulation. Figure 11 shows this function, which is accomplished by a simple first order filter consisting of R2 and C3. The cutoff frequency should be well above the highest modulating frequency and well below the receiver intermediate frequency.

The phase detector is the same as is used for phase-locked loops. It can be an analog multiplier (product detector) or a digital gate (either an AND or an exclusive-OR gate).

8.9 TRANSCEIVERS

A transceiver is simply a transmitter and receiver in one box. Transceivers are convenient and allow certain economies to be made. Most transceivers operate in the half-duplex mode.

8.9.1 HALF-DUPLEX TRANSCEIVERS

Many wireless communication systems use transceivers that switch from transmit to receive, either using a push-to-talk switch or voice-activated switching. In this case, it is often possible to use many components for both transmit and receive functions. Consider the VHF-FM transceiver whose block diagram is shown in Figure 12, for example.

Here, the CPU and the frequency synthesizer that it controls are used for both transmit and receive. When transmitting, the synthesizer doubles as carrier oscillator and FM modulator. When receiving, the synthesizer functions as the first local oscillator. Some transceivers also share audio circuitry.

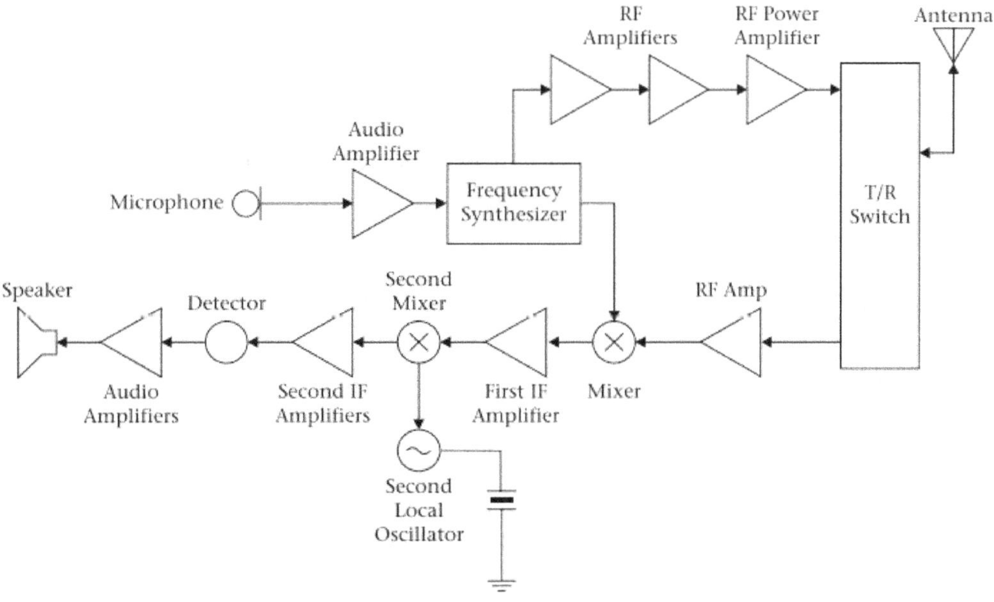

Fig: VHF-FM transceiver

Note that the receiver section of this transceiver uses double conversion; that is, there is a second local oscillator/mixer combination. The second local oscillator operates at a fixed frequency; the purpose of the second IF is to allow there to be a high first IF for good image rejection followed by a low second IF to simplify the design of a narrowband filter for good selectivity.

Half-duplex operation simplifies the connection of the transceiver to its antenna. A mechanical switch can be used, but as in the example, more often the switching is electronic. Since the antenna is never connected to both transmitter and receiver at the same time, there is no need for filters to separate transmitted and received signals.

8.9.2 MOBILE AND PORTABLE TELEPHONES

When full-duplex operation is required as it is with cordless and cellular telephones, it is necessary to use two separate channels, one each for transmit and receive. They must be far enough apart in frequency that a filter can separate them, so that the transmitter signal does not overload, and possibly damage, the receiver.

Figure 13 shows how this device, called a duplexer, fits into the system. Duplexers are also used at base stations to allow transmitters and receivers to use the same antenna simultaneously.

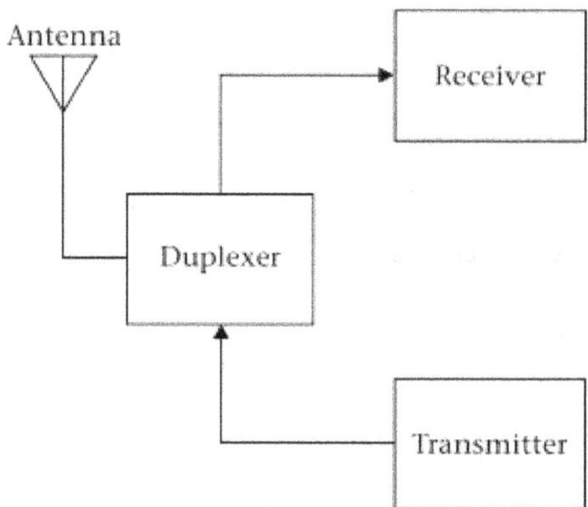

Fig: Use of duplexer for full-duplex communication

Chapter-9

Television

9.1 Television Fundamentals

The main concept of television is to transmit the sound and picture by radio wave. The output of consists of three technologies:

i. **TV camera:** Converts the sound and picture into electromagnetic signal
ii. **TV transmitter:** Sends the electromagnetic signal by radio wave with performing modulation.
iii. **TV receiver/set:** To reconstruct the sound and picture from electromagnetic signal.

9.2 Requirements of TV

To be successful, a television system may be required to reproduce faithfully

1) ***The shape of each object, or structural content:*** If only the structural content of each object in a scene were shown, we would have truly black-and-white TV (without any shades of gray).
2) ***The relative brightness of each object, or tonal content:*** If tonal content were added, we would have black-and-white still pictures.
3) ***Motion, or kinematic content and Sound:*** movies and talkies.
4) ***Color, or chromatic content:*** Color TV
5) ***Perspective, or stereoscopic content:*** This item is not essential. The next generation will Probably include it.

9.3 Formation of video

Video systems form pictures by scanning. The image is divided into a number of horizontal lines, which are traced in synchronously by the receiver and transmitter. The North American standard is 525 lines. European standard is 625 lines. To reproduce an image, the lines must be drawn quickly. The more quickly the lines are drawn, the less flicker that is present. The scan rates for North America and Europe are approximately 30 and 25 frames per second respectively.

9.4 Scanning process

Scanning is the process by which an electron beam spot is made to move across a rectangular area so as to cover it completely. This rectangular area may be the target surface in television camera or the screen of a picture tube in a television receiver. Former is the characteristic of transmitter scanning whereas the latter represents receiver scanning. The figure shows receiver scanning where the electron beam intensity modulated by the video signal scans the picture tube screen to reproduce the picture

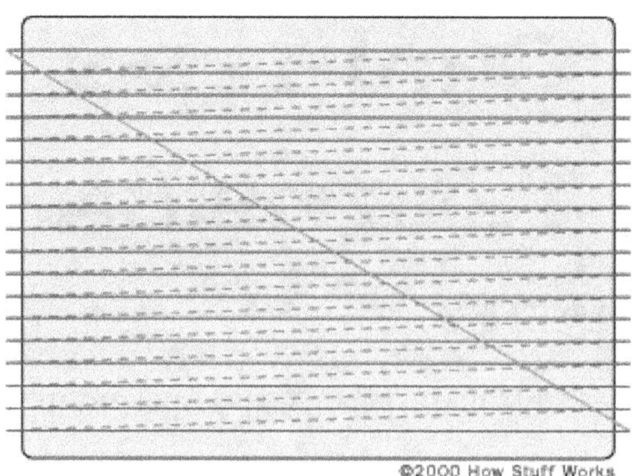

Fig: Scanning

1. Horizontal Scanning:

The movement of electron beam spot from left to right and back so as to start a new line in the same direction is termed as horizontal scanning. Horizontal scanning frequency is defined as the number of lines scanned per second.

Obviously in 625-line, 50 Hz system where 25 frames are transmitted per second, the horizontal scanning rate is 15625 lines per second. This is also termed as 15625 Hz because the signal that enables the spot scan horizontally at the rate of 15625Hz, as one cycle makes the spot scan from left extreme to right extreme.

2. Vertical Scanning

Vertical scanning is the movement of the electron beam spot in the vertical direction. Vertical scanning frequency may be defined as the number of views also called fields transmitted per second. The frequency of the vertical, scanning signal is 50 Hz. One cycle takes the spot from top to bottom (during trace) and back from bottom to top (during retrace).

3. Progressive scanning:

The television scene is first sampled in time to create frames, and within each frame all the raster lines are scanned from top to bottom. Almost all computer displays are sequentially scanned.

4. Interlaced scanning:

Frame rates of 25 or 30 Hz cause flicker. To reduce this, most television systems use a technique known as interlaced scan, which involves transmitting alternate lines of the picture, then returning and filling in the missing lines.

Each half of the picture is called a field, with the field rate being twice the frame rate. The electron beam that traces the picture is blanked during the time intervals in which the beam retraces its path. The time intervals where, blanking takes place are called the horizontal and vertical blanking intervals.

The lines that are scanned on the tube screen are produced by a narrow electron beam that is focused into a small 'spot' which is repeatedly moved across the screen, then progressively down it until the entire area has been covered (this is referred to as a 'raster'). The inside of the tube face is coated with a special phosphor that emits a bright light when bombarded with electrons.

By varying the strength of the beam the luminance of the spot can be controlled, thereby reproducing the various levels of contrast in our images. Colour television operates on the same principle, except that there are three separate beams and three colour phosphors, one for each of the primary colours Red Blue Green.

The spot is driven horizontally and vertically by two circuits called timebases. The Line Timebase moves the spot from left to right and the Field Timebase, from the top to the bottom. The video signal itself resets the timebases at the appropriate times to make the spot fly back from right to left and from the bottom to the top. This part of the raster scanning is called, appropriately, the flyback. The spot is turned off, or 'blanked' during flybacks. The Field Timebase scans very much slower than the Line Timebase.

The illustration below figure 2 shows how the interlaced raster is created. At the beginning of a frame the two timebases are both reset so that the spot is at position (A). Both timebases then start scanning. The video signal triggers line flybacks at the appropriate time until the end of the first field (odd) is reached.

Half-way through the last line (B), the field timebase is reset. The spot then flies back to (C), and continues with the remainder of the line, then scans all the even lines in a similar manner. Because the field timebase was reset half way through a line, the even field naturally interlaces between the lines of the odd field.

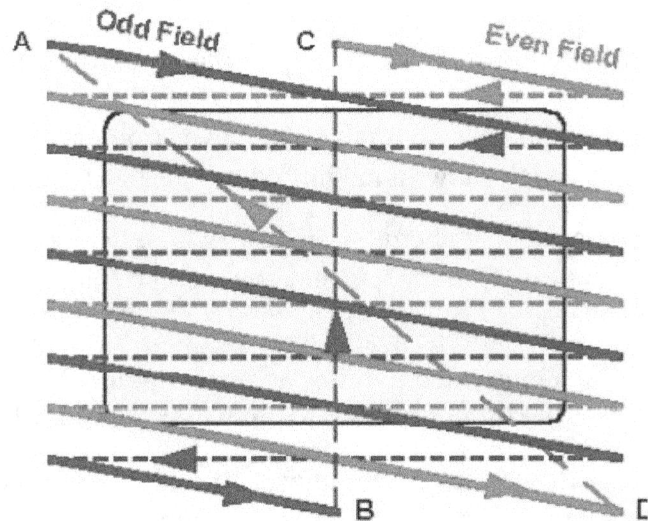

Fig: Interlaced Plan

When the spot reaches the end of the final line (D), both timebases are reset, and the spot flies back to (A), ready for the next frame.

This diagram gives the impression that the scan lines are at an angle. That is because so few lines are shown for clarity. In fact the angle is much less than 1 degree in reality, and is easily corrected by twisting the coils on the tube that deflect the electron beam.

The diagram also shows that the visible part of the screen is smaller than the area of the scanned raster. This is because it actually takes several line-scans for the frame timebase to fly back to the beginning (rather than the instantaneous paths shown for clarity on the diagram). The slight 'overscan' on the lines themselves also allows the spot time to stabilize before starting its active scan.

The PAL system comprises 625 lines, of which 574 are active. NTSC has 525 lines, of which 485 are active. During the time of inactive lines, it is customary to find non-image data stored in digital form. Examples of this are Teletext (Europe) and VITC timecode.

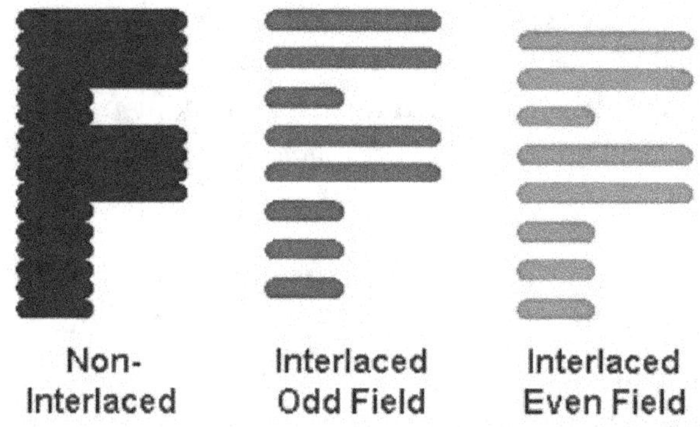

Fig: Formation of image in interlaced scanning

Interlacing then, is a very effective way of reducing the flicker on the picture without increasing the amount (known as 'bandwidth') of transmitted information. The problem is, it can sometimes produce an undesirable vertical 'bounce' on images that have strong horizontal detail. Look at the illustration shown in figure 3, which shows a magnified capital F, as it may appear on the screen.

As you can see, the non-interlaced character is stationary, whilst the interlaced version (separated here into its two fields) will appear to bounce up and down at the frame rate.

This is not a great problem with domestic televisions, because the viewing distance is so great and the spot is relatively 'soft'. On a video monitor at close quarters however, the effect is quite pronounced. That is why computer monitors are invariably non-interlaced.

Producers of TV graphics often attempt to minimize this effect by avoiding lots of horizontal detail and, where it is unavoidable, they use an odd number of lines for narrow horizontal features. This replaces the 'bounce' with a less obvious modulation in height.

9.5 COMPOSITE VIDEO SIGNAL

The composite video signal is the video signal into which blanking and synchronizing pulses are inserted at proper timings.

Composite video signal consists of a camera signal corresponds to desired picture information, blanking pulses to make the retraces invisible and synchronizing pulses to synchronize the transmitter and receiver scanning.

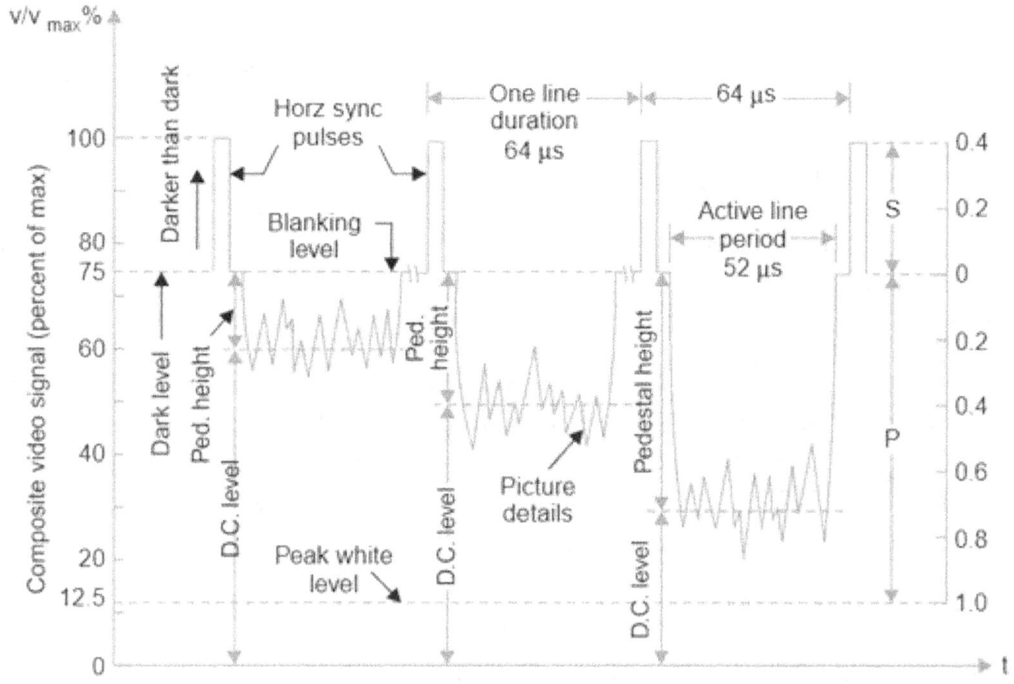

Fig: Composite video signal

Video signal of the composite video signal varies in between 10 % to 72 % levels. The 10 % level of the signal corresponds to the peak white level while the 72 % level of the signal corresponds to peak dark level. Gray shades are represented by the signals with the amplitude level varying in between 10 % and 72 % levels. Blanking pulses are placed from 72 % level to 75 % level. Sync pulses are placed from 75 % level to 100 % level (both vertical & horizontal during the blanking periods).

Peak White level: 10 to 12 % level is called peak white level because when video signal is having this amplitude a peak white spot is produced on the picture tube.

Peak Black level: 72% level is called black level. This level produces blackness on the raster.

Blanking level: 75 % level is called blanking level because the blanking pulses are inserted at this level.

Pedestal Height: The difference between blanking level and average brightness level is called pedestal height.

DC level or average brightness level: This level corresponds to the average value of the complete frame.

9.6 SYNCHRONIZATION

Synchronizing pulses added to the video signal at the end of every scan line and video frame ensure that the sweep oscillators in the receiver remain locked in step with the transmitted signal, so that the image can be reconstructed on the receiver screen.

A sync separator circuit detects the sync voltage levels and sorts the pulses into horizontal and vertical sync.

1. Horizontal synchronization

The horizontal synchronization pulse (horizontal sync HSYNC), separates the scan lines. The horizontal sync signal is a single short pulse which indicates the start of every line. The rest of the scan line follows, with the signal ranging from 0.3 V (black) to 1 V (white), until the next horizontal or vertical synchronization pulse.

The format of the horizontal sync pulse varies. In the 525-line NTSC system it is a 4.85 μs-long pulse at 0 V. In the 625-line PAL system the pulse is 4.7 μs synchronization pulse at 0 V . This is lower than the amplitude of any video signal (blacker than black) so it can be detected by the level-sensitive "sync stripper" circuit of the receiver.

2. Vertical synchronization

Vertical synchronization (Also vertical sync or VSYNC) separates the video fields. In PAL and NTSC, the vertical sync pulse occurs within the vertical blanking interval. The vertical sync pulses are made by prolonging the length of HSYNC pulses through almost the entire length of the scan line.

The vertical sync signal is a series of much longer pulses, indicating the start of a new field. The sync pulses occupy the whole of line interval of a number of lines at the beginning and end of a scan; no picture information is transmitted during vertical retrace. The pulse sequence is designed to allow horizontal sync to continue during vertical retrace; it also indicates whether each field represents even or odd lines in interlaced systems (depending on whether it begins at the start of a horizontal line, or mid-way through).

9.7 BLANKING PULSE

During scanning process of every horizontal line the electron beam is deflected from right to left for retrace. During retrace period no video signal is applied to the cathode of the picture tube, but the electron beam from the cathode will strike the picture tube screen to produce a bright white horizontal line. Similarly at the end of the every field there is a vertical retrace.

During this period also electron beam can strike the screen to produce bright vertical line. So to avoid this retrace period, the retrace line should be made invisible. For this purpose we are sending blanking pulses along with the video signal, from the transmitter to the receiver.

In TV, 'blanking' means 'going to black' as part of the video signal, the blanking voltage is at the black level. Video voltage at the black level cuts off the beam currents in the picture tube to black out the light from screen. The purpose of providing the blanking pulses is to make invisible the retraces of the scanning process. The horizontal blanking pulse at the frequency of 15625 Hz, blanks out the retrace from right to left for each line. The vertical blanking pulses at 50 Hz blank out the retrace from bottom to top for each field.

9.8 FRONT PORCH AND BACK PORCH

The front porch is a brief (about 1.5 microsecond) period inserted between the end of each transmitted line of picture and the leading edge of the next line sync pulse. Its purpose was to allow voltage levels to stabilize in older televisions, preventing interference between picture lines. The front porch is the first component of the horizontal blanking interval which also contains the horizontal sync pulse and the back porch.

The back porch is the portion of each scan line between the end (rising edge) of the horizontal sync pulse and the start of active video. It is used to restore the black level (300 mV.) reference in analog video. In signal processing terms, it compensates for the fall time and settling time following the sync pulse.

9.9 EQUALIZING PULSES

Synchronization pulses of double frequency and of short period leading and following the vertical sync. Proper equalizing pulses are needed for picture stability on the screen, for proper vertical deflection, interlacing and for PAL switch generation. Missing or distorted equalizing pulses can cause misalignment of the video image on the screen, skewing effect, color distortion and loss.

A narrow pulse superimposed on the vertical blanking pulse of a composite television signal before and after the vertical synchronizing pulse. Equalizing pulses are added to the synchronizing signal in interlaced scanning in order to eliminate the difference in the form of the odd and even vertical synchronizing pulses; the difference in form, which appears when the vertical synchronizing pulses are extracted from the synchronizing signal by means of an integrated filter, is due to the different location of the line synchronizing pulses.

The duration of an equalizing pulse is approximately 2.5 microseconds, and the repetition frequency is twice the line frequency. The number of equalizing pulses depends on the identity requirements for the even and odd vertical synchronizing pulses and is usually five or six.

9.10 TELEVISION SYSTEMS AND STANDARDS

There are five essentially different television systems in use around the world. The two main ones are the American [Federal Communications Commission (FCC) system for monochrome and National Television Standards Committee (NTSC) system for color] and the European [Comite Consultatif International de Radio (CCIR) system for monochrome and Phase Alternation by Line (PAL) system for color.]

STANDARD	AMERICAN SYSTEM	EUROPEAN SYSTEM
Number of lines per frame	525	625
Number of frames per second	30	25
Field frequency, Hz	60	50
Line frequency, Hz	15,750	15,625
Channel width, MHz	6	7
Video bandwidth, MHz	4.2	5
Color subcarrier, MHz	3.58*	4.43*
Sound system	FM	FM
Maximum sound deviation, kHz	25	50
Intercarrier frequency, MHz	4.5	5.5

Table: Selected Standards of Major Television Systems

9.11 BLACK & WHITE TELEVISION TRANSMITTER

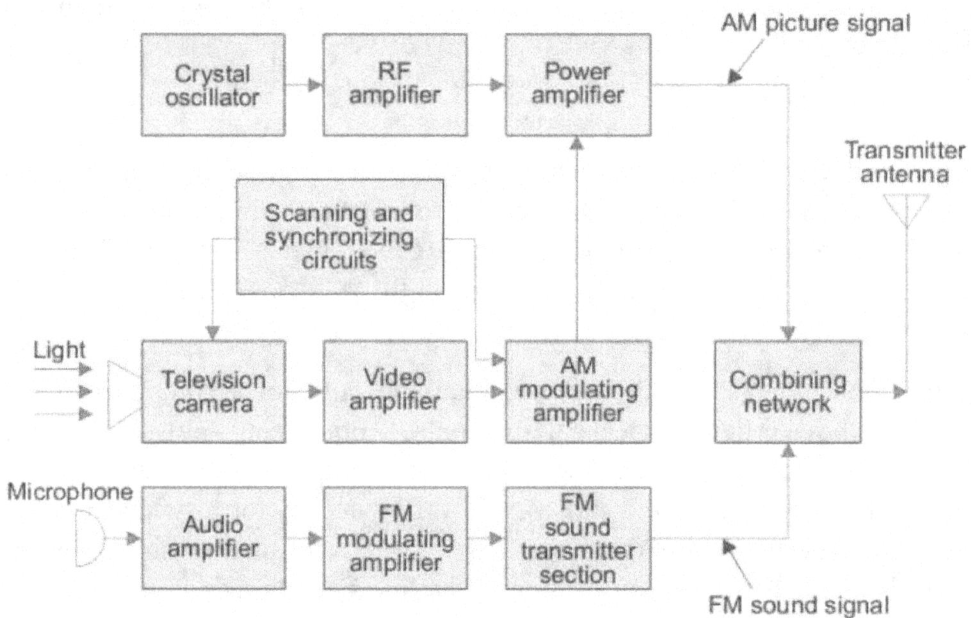

Fig: Black & White TV Transmitter

A block diagram of a monochrome television transmitter system is shown in figure 5. A separate transmitter is used for sound, connected to the same antenna as the picture transmitter.

The continuous wave (CW) sine wave output is given large amplification before feeding to the power amplifier where its amplitude is made to vary (AM) in accordance with the modulating signal received from the modulating amplifier. The modulated output is combined (see Fig. 5) with the frequency modulated (FM) sound signal in the combining network and then fed to the transmitting antenna for radiation.

The luminance signal from the camera is amplified and synchronizing pulses added before feeding it to the modulating amplifier. Synchronizing pulses are transmitted to keep the camera and the picture tube beams in step. The allotted picture carrier frequency is generated by a crystal controlled oscillator.

9.12 BLACK & WHITE TELEVISION RECEIVER

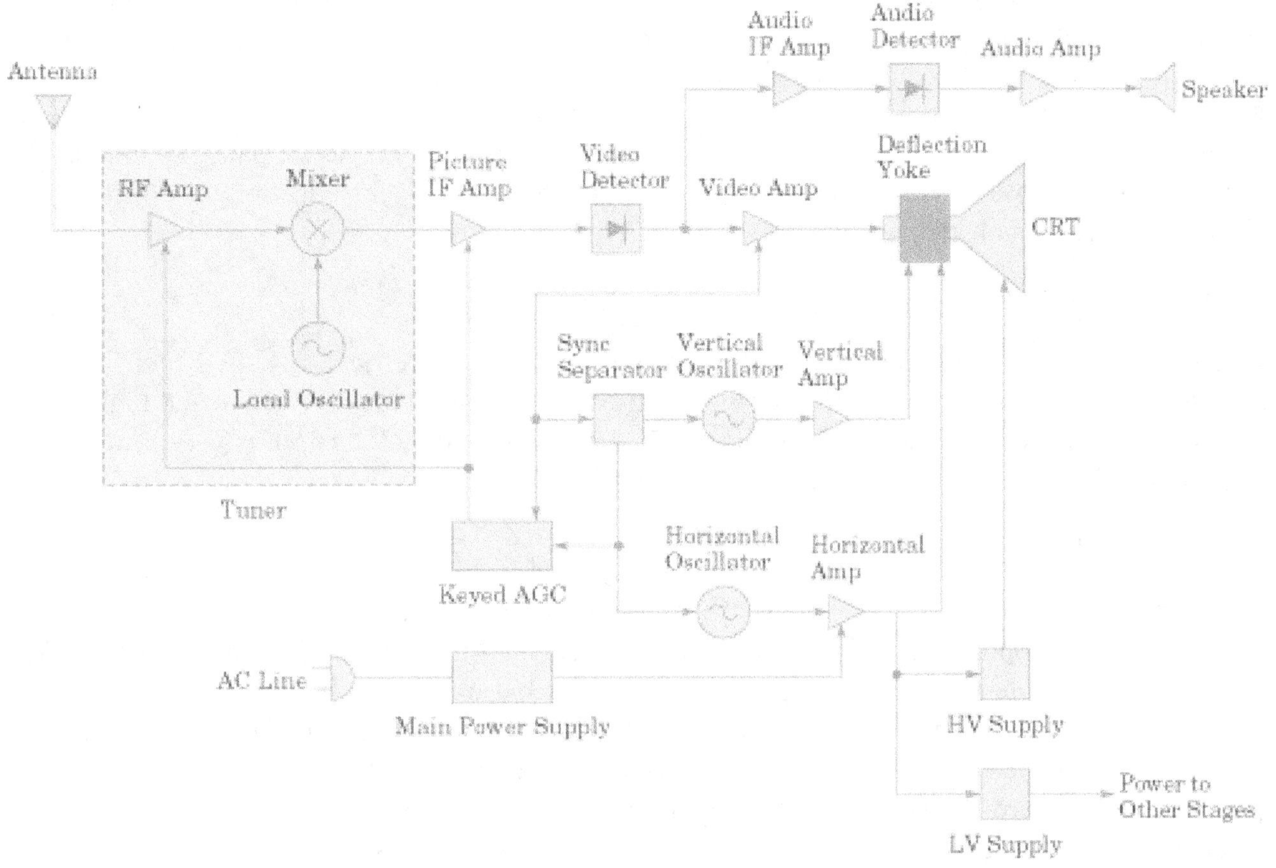

Fig: Black & white TV receiver

In a typical black and white television receiver (figure 6), the signal from the antenna is fed to the tuner. Two channel selector switches – one for the VHF (very-high-frequency) channels and the other for the UHF (ultra-high-frequency) channels are used. They connect circuits that are tuned to the desired channels and, also discriminate against signals from undesired channels.

The amplified signals from the desired channel are then passed to the mixer, which transposes all the signal frequencies in the channel to different values, called intermediate frequencies. The output of the tuner consists of all the signals in the desired channel, but the intermediate channel is fixed in the frequency band from 41 to 47 MHz, no matter what channel is tuned in. This is kind of like those cable television "set top" converters, that, regardless of what channel you're watching, always convert it to "channel 3" for your TV set.

From the tuner, the 41-47 MHz channel with all picture and sound information present is passed successively through several additional amplifiers (from two to four intermediate frequency, or IF, amplifiers), which provide most of the amplification in the receiver. Their amplification is automatically adjusted, being maximum on a weak signal and less on a strong signal. So far the receiver handles the signals in the channel just like they would be received from the transmitter, except for the shift to intermediate frequencies and the amplification.

The next stage is the video detector, which removes the high frequency carrier signal and recovers the video signal. The detector also reproduces (at a lower frequency) the sound carrier and its frequency variations. The sound signal is then separated from the picture signal and passes through a frequency detector, which recovers the audio signal. This signal is amplified further and fed to the loudspeaker, where it re-creates the accompanying sound. The picture signal from the video detector is used in the normal fashion for display on the CRT of the television receiver.

1. Antenna:

Antenna converts electromagnetic waves in to corresponding electrical signals. It consists of a dipole with one reflector and two or more directors are used. It is a compact high again directional array is often used in firings areas. In areas where signal strength is very low booster amplifiers with suitable matching networks are used.

2. A Transmission Line:

A transmission line connects antenna to the front end of the T.V. Receiver i.e. R.F Tuner and its impendence is 300ohms. Twin lead is generally used for this purpose. Its impendence is 300 ohms. Folded dipole also has an impendence close to 300 ohms. For maximum signal transfer the impendence of the antenna and the receiver's end both should match. This is done with the help of a impendence balancing transformer known as 'balun. Thus if the impendence is matched properly 500 micro volts to 1 mV signal strength is achieved. Thus using antenna all electromagnetic waves are converted into electrical signals and these are then coupled to turner through a transmission line.

3. RF Section:

This section consists of RF amplifier mixer and local oscillator. This is normally mounted on a spate is called the front end or RF tuner. According to frequency of reception these are VHF tuner and UHF signals picked up by the antenna. Here the receiver uses the super heterodyning principle for conversion of the incoming signal into the common fixed carrier frequencies called Intermediate Frequencies. These are picture IF and sound IF. These values are 38.9 MHz for picture VIF and 33.4 MHz for sound SIF. Thus using RF section or channel selector or RF Tuner we can amplify the incoming composite video signal to the required level and then these are further converted into the VIF and SIF. Further these are fed the video IF amplifier.

Thus the main function of the turner is as follows.

i. To selected channel signal from the many signals up by the Antenna and reject others.
ii. To amplify the received or selected signal.
iii. To convent the incoming signal frequency to a common IF band.

iv.   To provide good S/N ratio.

v.   It avoids adjacent channel frequency.

vi.   It provides image frequency rejection.

vii.   It acts as coupling device between antenna & receiver.

viii.   It prevents spurious picks ups from sources which operate in the IF band of receiver.

ix.   It has a fine control for accurate setting in the IF band.

4. Video IF Amplifier:

Since the composite video signals is the envelope of the modulated pictures IF signal practically all the gain and selectivity of the receiver is provided by the IF section. Generally 3 or 4 IF transistors amplifier stages are used for this purpose. In integral circuits one IC contains all the IF amplifier stages.

The main functions of the IF sections

i.   To amplify the modulated IF signals over its entire bandwidths.

ii.   It also provides vestigial side band correction.

iii.   It provides again of above 800 to amplify the 0.5 mV input signal to about 4 v.

iv.   It also provides adjacent channel signal rejection.

v.   It also provides good selectivity.

5. Video detectors:

Modulated IF selections after due amplification in the IF selection are fed to the video detector. The detector is designed to receive the CVS and to transform the sound signal to another lower carrier frequency. This is done by rectifying the input signals and filtering out unwanted frequency components. Thus the video signal which is demodulated with correct polarity is fed to the cathode of picture tube after one stage of video amplification.

6. Video Amplifier:

The picture tube needs video signal with peak amplitude of 80 to 100 V for producing picture with good contrast. This amplifier provides necessary gain to achieve necessary amplification to the video signal to drive the picture tube. Here gain control is also provides in the stage to adjust the contrast between black and white parts of the picture. That's why this gain control is also known as contrast control. Thus the amplified video signals are fed to the cathode of the picture tube.

7. Sound Signal Separation:

The picture and sound signals on their respective carrier are amplified together in the IF section. In video detector VIF of 38.9 MHz acts as carrier and beats with the sound carrier 33.4 MHz produce a difference of 5.5 MHz. This is called inter carrier signals. This retains all the FM modulated sound signals by providing a resonant tarp circuit in the video detector the sound signals is separated from the video detector.

8. Sound Section:

The sound section consists sound IF amplifier, FM detector, Audio voltage amplifier, audio power amplifier and loud speaker. The inter carrier sound IF signal directly cannot drive the FM detector. So, at least one stage of amplification is needed to drive the FM detector. This is achieved with the sound IF amplifier. After amplification the sound IF signal is fed to FM detectors. The FM detector is normally a ratio detector or discriminator proceeded by a limiter. Here in this stage sound is demodulated and De-emphasis restores the amplitudes of higher audio frequencies to their correct level. Thus demodulated sound signal is further amplified using voltage amplifiers in order to drive power amplifier. The power amplifier is either single ended or a push pull amplifier employing Transistors. These stages provide volume and tone controls. Thus amplified signals are fed to loud speaker. Finally loud speaker converts electrical signal into corresponding sound signal.

9. Picture Tube Circuitry and Control:

The output from the video amplifier may be fed to cathode. The cathode emits this video output by the application of the thermionic emission. This emitted electron from an electron beam. This electron beam moves with phosphor. This electron beam moves towards screen and strikes the screen of the picture tube which is coated with phosphor. Thus when electron beam touches the phasporaous screen it emits light. If this electron beam is deflected horizontally and vertically by the application of deflection coils and circuits it produces raster on the screen. Thus using picture tube and its circuitry electrical signal can be converted into corresponding picture information.

10. AGC:

AGC means automatic gain control. AGC circuit control gain of RF and IF stages to deliver almost constant signal voltage to the video detector, despite changes in the signal picked up by the Antenna. Generally the signal available from the antenna to the television receiver may vary from fraction of a m V to fraction of volt. It is clear that the television receiver's gain will vary with these variations in the signal strength. The result variation in gain is that a strong signal will produces excessive contrast, if the signal is very strong it over loads the video IF stage. This results in clipping is sync pulse tips. As a result sync pulse will be lost and the picture will appear turnout and will roll vertically. Over loading of the video stage produces negative picture. In order to prevent the above we require a circuit that control the output of the video detector to produce a good picture is known as AGC. The main advantages of AGC are as

i. Intensity and contrast of the picture once set remains constant irrespective of changes in the input signal strength.
ii. Contrast in the reproduced picture does not change when the receiver is switched from one situation to another.
iii. Amplitude cross modulation distortion on strong signals is avoided.
iv. Further due to passing aero planes and fading effects will be reduced.
v. The sound signal being the part of CVS also stays constants as it is also controlled by the AGC.
vi. Separation of sync pulses becomes easy.

vii.   The gain on weak signals is improved using delayed AGC.

11. Sync separator:

The horizontal and vertical sync pulses that from the part of the composite video signal are separated in the sync separator. The CVS is either taken from the video detector output or after one stage of video amplification. A sync separator is clipper circuit that is suitably biased to produce output only during sync pulse amplitude of the video signal.

12. Sync processing and AFC circuit:

The output obtained from the sync separators is fed simultaneously to a differentiator and integrator circuits. The differentiator provides sharp pulse for triggering the horizontal Oscillator. Thus using integrator and differentiator vertical sync pulsed are separated from the sync separators.

As the differentiator is a high pass filter it also developed output in response to noise pulses in addition to the spiked horizontal sync pulses. These results in occasional wrong triggering to the horizontal oscilator, which results in diagonal tearing of the reproduced picture. This problem can be solved by using automatic frequency control circuit.

The AFC circuit employs a discrimination arrangement which compares the incoming horizontal sync pulses and the voltage that develops across the output of the horizontal deflection amplifier. Thus the AFC output is a dc control voltage that is free of noise pulses. This control voltage is used to synchronize the horizontal oscillator with the received horizontal sync pulses.

13. Vertical deflection Circuit:

Blocking oscillators are normally used as vertical deflection oscillators. This oscillators produce necessary saw tooth voltages required for vertical deflection. A potentiometer frequency known as vertical hold is used in this section to reset the vertical oscillators frequency from it frequency drift. The output of the oscillators is fed to a power amplifier. After amplification the same output is coupled to vertical deflections coils to produce the vertical deflection of the beam on the picture tube screen.

14. Horizontal deflection circuit:

The horizontal oscillator is similar to vertical oscillators. It is used develop sweep derive voltage at 15625 Hz. This oscillator is controlled by the control voltage developed by the AFC circuit. The oscillator output is wave shaped to produce linear rise of current in the horizontal deflection coils. Since the deflection coils need about one amp of current to sweep the entire raster, for this purpose the output of the oscillator is given one stage to power amplification and then fed to the horizontal deflection coils.

15. High Voltage Supply (EHT):

In black and white tubes anode requires a voltage of 15KV for sufficient brightness. This is known as HV or EHT(extra high tension supply). This high voltage is produced during retrace intervals of horizontals scanning. A high voltage pulses of amplitude between 6 to 9 kV are developed across the primary winding of the horizontal output transformer. Further these are stepped up by an auto transformer winding to about 10 to 15 KV and then fed to high voltage rectifier. The output of the rectifier is filtered to provide required dc voltage. This is fed to final anode of the picture tube.

16. Low Voltage Power Supply:

The usual B+ or low voltage supply is obtained by rectifying an filtering the arc. mains supply. This gives to various sections of the receivers. Thus a T.V Receiver can convert CVS signals in to corresponding picture and sound signal.

9.13 CATHODE RAY TUBE

Construction:

The components of a monochrome CRT includes:

1) The electron gun emits a beam of electrons
2) The control grid regulates brightness
3) The screen grid (first anode)
4) The focus grid (in combination with the screen grid) forms an electronic lens
5) The ultor (second anode) is used to avoid arcing

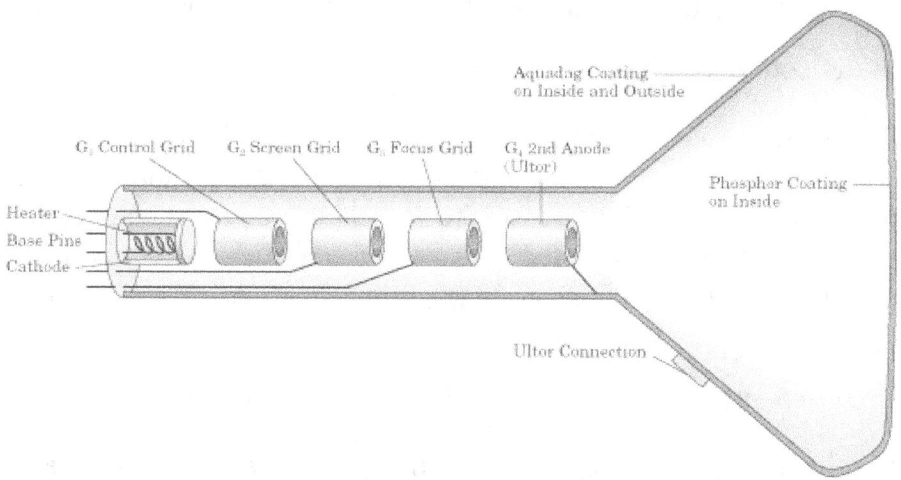

Fig: Cathode Ray Tube

Operation:

The operation of a CRT monitor is basically very simple. In a cathode ray tube (figure 7), the "cathode" is a heated filament (not unlike the filament in a normal light bulb). The heated filament is in a vacuum created inside a glass "tube." The "ray" is a stream of electrons that naturally pour off a heated cathode into the vacuum.

Electrons are negative. The anode is positive, so it attracts the electrons pouring off the cathode. In a TV's cathode ray tube, the stream of electrons is focused by a focusing anode into a tight beam and then accelerated by an accelerating anode. This tight, high-speed beam of electrons flies through the vacuum in the tube and hits the flat screen at the other end of the tube. This screen is coated with phosphor, which glows when struck by the beam.

A cathode ray tube consists of one or more electron guns, possibly internal electrostatic deflection plates and a phosphor target. CRT has three electron beams – one for each (Red, Green, and Blue). The electron beam produces a tiny, bright visible spot when it strikes the phosphor-coated screen. In every monitor device the entire front area of the tube is scanned repetitively and systematically in a fixed pattern called a raster. An image (raster) is displayed by scanning the electron beam across the screen. The phosphor's targets are begins to fade after a short time, the image needs to be refreshed continuously. Thus CRT produces the three color images which are primary colors.

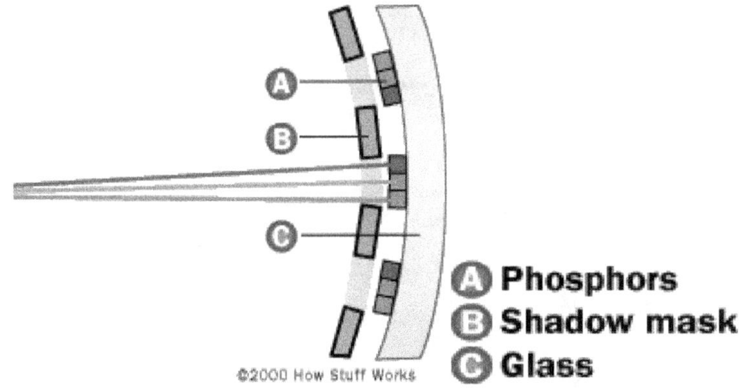

Fig: Color cathode ray tube

Color CRTs must have 3 electron guns to reproduce the 3 primary colors (figure 8). The three video signals are applied to the electron guns, one to each gun. Each gun illuminates a different type of phosphor that glow red, green, and blue. Adjustments include: Purity and Convergence.

ELECTRON GUN

Inside a CRT, a device known as an electron gun (which consists of a negative electrode, or cathode), a series of computer windings known as steering coils and a heater generate a beam of electrons. The steering coils create a magnetic field, which guides the beam so that it scans back and forth across the screen, starting at the top. Air is withdrawn from the CRT so that air molecules don't interfere with the passage of electrons between the electron gun and the screen.

PHOSPHOR

Phosphor is the name given to any substance that emits visible light when exposed to radiation, such as ultraviolet light, or, in this case, a beam of electrons. The electrons collide with the phosphor atoms, causing them to gain energy or become "excited." When the phosphor atoms lose the energy gained during the collisions, they emit particles, or photons, of visible light.

BLACK-AND-WHITE AND COLOR

Older CRT TVs use just a single color phosphor and so can only produce black-and-white, or monochrome, pictures. Later CRT TVs use phosphors colored in the three primary colors -- red, green and blue -- and therefore can produce full color pictures. In the latter case, manufacturers apply multiple color coatings to the screen through a device known as an aperture mask, made from perforated metal, to create thousands of narrow, colored lines of phosphor.

9.14 COLOR TELEVISION RECEIVER

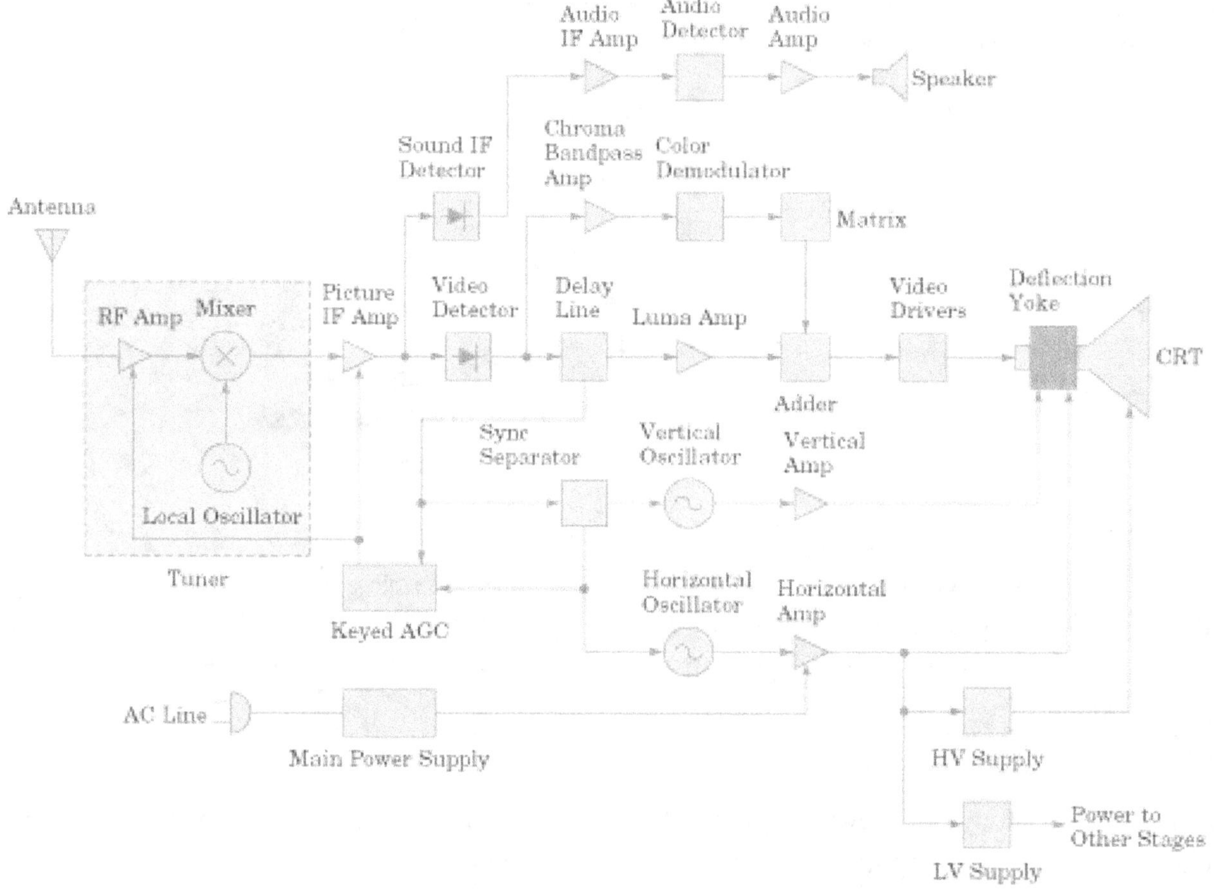

Fig: Color TV receiver

> Color-signal processing is similar in that the tuner and video IF sections are similar to those in a monochrome receiver, as is the audio section (except that color receivers are likely to have stereo sound)
> The differences lie in the way the chroma signal is demodulated and the result is combined with the luma.

> There is also a separate IF detector for sound
> The chroma signal must be separated from the luma and sent to the color demodulators, typically using a comb filter

9.15 TELEVISION RECEIVER TROUBLESHOOTING

Typical problems in a television receiver include:

> No Raster
> No Video and/or Audio
> Synchronization Problems

Signal Tracing and Injection are used as troubleshooting aids in television systems